DINWIDDIE COUNTY VIRGINIA

A BRIEF HISTORY

RONALD R. SEAGRAVE

THE History PRESS

Published by The History Press
Charleston, SC 29403
www.historypress.net

First published 2012

Manufactured in the United States

ISBN 978.1.60949.784.2

Library of Congress CIP data applied for.

CONTENTS

ACKNOWLEDGEMENTS

Giving credit where it is due is one of an author's more satisfying duties—provided one is confident that he has left no one out. In this instance, I approach the task with no such confidence, nor glee. The information collected here has been garnered over a period of some five years and is the product of scores of reference sources. First, I wish to thank Laura Willoughby for agreeing to write the foreword to this work. Her abilities as a professional museum curator and author and her regional knowledge made her a logical choice. Next, I would like to thank Adam Ferrell, publishing director of The History Press, for proceeding with this work during this period in our history. The writing and compiling of any Virginia history would not be possible without the outstanding resources of Virginia Department of Historic Resources, the Virginia Historical Society and the Library of Virginia. We are all fortunate to have most of the *Virginia Gazette* issues online at http://research.history.org/DigitalLibrary/BrowseVG.cfm, which allows us to see how regional information was once passed along in the eighteenth century. For example, the *Virginia Gazette* was the principal source of the information paraphrased herein on Benjamin Woodward, the counterfeiter, as well as the various American Civil War period newspapers that covered who flanked who and the men lost.

I wish to personally thank Diane Dallmeyer, of the Chesterfield History Society; Kristy Fowler, of Pamplin Historical Park; Ann Blumenschine, of the Petersburg National Battlefield; Bryan Pierce, general manager of Virginia Motorsports Park; and Kevin Kirby, director of tourism for the City of Petersburg, for his assistance and review of the "Attractions Every Visitor Should Find of Interest" section herein, ensuring its completeness.

Lastly, I would like to thank Linda Cummingham, vice-president of the Bank of McKenney, and Kevin Messengill, administrator for Dinwiddie County, for their encouragement and professionalism, as well as the Dinwiddie Clerk's Office for the use of Isham E. Hargrave's map of Dinwiddie County, which included the town of Petersburg, circa 1820. I would finally like to thank Charlotte Ragsdale, Mary Bettie Form, Amy Lynn Williams and Curtis Anderson for their assistance and encouragement.

Any additions and corrections may be added or seen by going to http://dinwiddiecountyhistory.blogspot.co.uk/.

FOREWORD

Dinwiddie County was officially established in 1752 when Prince George County was divided in two. The county was named for Robert Dinwiddie, the lieutenant governor for the colony of Virginia from 1751 to 1758, who was born in Glasgow, Scotland, in 1692. Dinwiddie began his career in Bermuda as a commodities trader, merchant and shipbuilder. His first official appointment with Great Britain was in 1721 when he was appointed to a post charged with policing customs transactions in Bermuda, Barbados and the West Indies. By the 1740s, Dinwiddie had become an advisor to British parliament and Great Britain's Board of Trade on matters concerning the nation's colonies. It is ironic that the county's namesake was recognized as a trade expert, as much of Dinwiddie County's history centers on the exchange and transport of goods and services.

The creation of Bristol Parish in 1643 by the Anglican Church is a testament to the fact that an increasingly large number of settlers were populating land in the region by the third quarter of the seventeenth century. Two years after the formation of Bristol Parish, Fort Henry was established adjacent to the Appomattox River. Established as a defense against Native Americans, Fort Henry became a starting point for expeditions organized to explore land in present-day Dinwiddie County and beyond. By the 1650s, trade with Native Americans was flourishing. Fort Henry was the center for this early commerce.

It is estimated that more than five hundred militiamen from Dinwiddie County saw service during the Revolutionary War. Fighting reached the county in April 1781, when British troops led by Benedict Arnold and Major

General William Phillips clashed with troops, including many local militiamen defending Petersburg. The British troops set fire to tobacco being stored in warehouses before retreating across the Appomattox River. The following month, Phillips returned to Petersburg, occupying Bollingbrook, the residence of Robert Bolling III's widow, Mary Marshall Tabb Bolling. On May 10, troops under the command of Lafayette shelled British forces from across the river. Three days later, Phillips died of a fever at Bollingbrook. On May 20, General Cornwallis traveled through Dinwiddie, most likely on what is now Halifax Road, reuniting with Phillips's troops now under the command of Benedict Arnold. From Petersburg, the ill-fated British army marched on toward Yorktown, where it would ultimately surrender to American forces.

From the time of the first settlements to the years leading up to the Civil War, agriculture dominated Dinwiddie's economy. Petersburg, a city within Dinwiddie County until the municipality became independent in 1850, thrived in part due to the volume of tobacco and other crops grown in Dinwiddie that were brought to the city to be processed, sold and transported to cities up and down the eastern seaboard. While Petersburg's economy was dependent on Dinwiddie's agricultural output, Dinwiddie's upper-class planters relied on Petersburg's artisans to supply them with goods. Petersburg's craftsmen divided their time fulfilling commissions for city and county folks, producing wares such as furniture, silver and horse carriages.

Even before the Revolutionary War, the westward migration of settlers brought a demand for slave labor to the region. In addition to cultivating crops, slaves engaged in other forms of manual labor, such as clearing forests and building dams for mills. Between 1782 and 1806, 120 slaves were freed in Dinwiddie as a result of more relaxed manumission laws. Many of these freemen and women settled in Petersburg.

The first census undertaken in 1790 showed Dinwiddie with a population of 7,334 slaves and 6,036 whites. By the 1820s, both white city and county dwellers saw the advantage of a large number of slaves who were used not just for crop production but also leased out to Petersburg artisans and manufacturers. During this era, the free African American population of Petersburg continued to grow. In 1830, 2,032 free African Americans were living in Petersburg, and 858 resided in Dinwiddie County. By 1850, the year Petersburg became an independent city, its free black population surpassed that of any other city in Virginia.

The advent of railroads in Dinwiddie further increased commerce for the region. The Petersburg Railroad was incorporated in 1830. By 1833, the sixty-mile route traversed Dinwiddie County from Petersburg and terminated in Weldon, North Carolina. Five years later, the railroad established connections with lines to major North Carolina cities, further opening up the markets between the region and North Carolina. In 1854, the South Side Railroad was completed. This rail line provided an east–west route through the county, terminating at Lynchburg and Petersburg. The county's rail lines would play a strategic role during the Civil War.

Numerous Dinwiddie men enlisted in local volunteer companies to fight for the Confederacy. These companies included the Dinwiddie Cavalry, the Cockade Cavalry, the Cockade Rifles and the Dinwiddie Grays. Dinwiddie women and children were left behind to man the homefront. Local women participated in the Soldiers' Relief Society making bandages and clothing for soldiers.

In 1864, the first Civil War battles in the area were fought on Dinwiddie soil. Assaults by the Union army, such as the Wilson-Kautz raid and the Battle of Reams Station, were aimed at destroying the county's railroads, key supply lines for Confederate troops. By the winter of 1865, both sides were entrenched in forts located around the circumference of Petersburg. General Lee occupied the Turnbell House in eastern Dinwiddie County from November 1864 until April 1865.

The Battles of Hatcher's Run, Dinwiddie Courthouse, Sutherland and Five Forks had troops on opposing sides vying for control of the siege lines. Finally on April 2, 1865, the Union offensive broke through Lee's lines. The surrender of Petersburg and ultimately Richmond followed. This was the prelude to the end of the Civil War.

The 150 years after the end of the war saw eras of poverty and prosperity for Dinwiddie County. The Great Depression, World Wars I and II and the civil rights movement, milestones in American history, impacted Dinwiddie County citizens as well. Technological innovations such as the advent of the automobile also had an effect on the local population as a major interstate was built through the county. Through it all, Dinwiddie County residents have cultivated the land, established businesses and industries and enjoyed leisurely activities at county parks, lakes and ball fields.

Images included in this volume provide a record of Dinwiddie County's history. Historical milestones as well as everyday activities documenting people, places and events are featured. What follows is a rich visual history of a county steeped in American history, a history that all Dinwiddie residents should be proud of.

Laura Willoughby, Curator of Collections
Petersburg Museums, Petersburg, Virginia

INTRODUCTION

When a small band of adventurers from the ships *Susan Constant*, *Godspeed* and *Discovery* landed their shallop in the "Countrey of Apamatica" on May 8, 1607, they set foot upon territory that may have been in present-day Dinwiddie County. These men would establish the first permanent English settlement in the New World at Jamestown. Here, Captain Christopher Newport and his crew who dared to cross the Atlantic in search of fame and fortune met the Appomattox Indians and their queen, Opussoquionuske, described first as a "fat, lusty, manly woman" and later as "a comely young savage." Because this point of land made by the confluence of the James and Appomattox Rivers seemed too exposed a place for safety, the pioneers remained but four days. Then retracing their course, they finally settled at Jamestown. The seating of land, therefore, in the area later to become Dinwiddie was not accomplished for a number of years. From 1702 until 1752, the history of Dinwiddie County is linked to that of Prince George County. Before 1702, both Dinwiddie and Prince George Counties were part of Charles City County, created in 1634. The British Virginia General Assembly formally incorporated both Petersburg and adjacent Blandford on December 17, 1748. Wittontown, north of the river, was settled in 1749 and became incorporated as Pocahontas in 1752. Petersburg was enlarged slightly in 1762, adding twenty-eight acres to "Old Town."

Dinwiddie County was established on May 1, 1752, while still under British rule, from Prince George County. Early on, Dinwiddie County included Petersburg, while the adjacent village of Blandford remained for the time being in Prince George County. Dinwiddie County today shares its borders with Amelia, Nottoway, Brunswick, Greensville, Sussex, Prince George and Chesterfield Counties, as well as with the independent city of Petersburg.

Its earliest inhabitants were nomadic hunter-gatherers who followed the early animal migrations prior to 8000 BC; these were the Paleo-Indians. In 1947, America's largest Paleo-Indian workshop site was discovered here, as well as hundreds of various stone tools and arrowheads of later periods in various fields and streams throughout the county. As the European settlers came to Dinwiddie County in the seventeenth century, some were Loyalists with their vested land grants from the King of England. Others were just looking for a better life and had little. Unfortunately, all too many were brought here as slaves. However, all came with diverse cultural, political and social values and views. Adding to the mix were the various religious views of the settlers, varying from African spiritualism to Quakerism and to those that were supported by the King's Church. By the time the American Revolution arrived, Dinwiddie County had grown to where it was able to raise several militia units that would fight to expel the county from the yoke of British rule. But not all shared that view; some remained Loyalist, while others stayed neutral.

Dinwiddie County has been the birthplace of a number of noted individuals. Dixon Hall Lewis, an American politician who later would serve as a representative and a senator from Alabama, was born on Bothwick plantation. Winfield Scott was born at Laurel Branch in 1786. One of Scott's earliest schoolmasters was James Hargrove, a local Quaker, who labored hard to curb the passion and mold the character of young Winfield to usefulness and virtue. This esteemed small man was highly respected by his pupils. Scott later attended the College of William and Mary, studied law in the office of a private attorney and served as a Virginia militia cavalry corporal near Petersburg in 1807. He went on to have a most distinguished military career. Alfred Jefferson Vaughan Jr., born in 1830, was an American civil engineer, planter, soldier and writer. Fitz Lee was born in Dinwiddie, a "Buffalo Soldier" in the U.S. Army and a recipient of America's highest military decoration, the Medal of Honor, for his actions in the Spanish-American War. Robert Boisseau Pamplin, born in 1911, was an American businessman and philanthropist.

Dinwiddie County is considered a major part of what was often called "Southside Virginia" and once maintained a large enslaved and a limited free black population prior to the American Civil War. This gave rise to several unlikely souls of note. Elizabeth Keckley was born into slavery by her master and father, Armistead Burwell. Later in life, she worked for Mrs. Jefferson Davis as her dressmaker. She was allowed to purchase her own freedom and went to work for Mary Todd Lincoln. Her son would fight for the Union army as a white man and lose his life in combat. Thomas Day learned his father's carpentry trade and became a well-known free black cabinetmaker at Milton, North Carolina. He saw to it that his children were raised in private schools back east by providing their tuition and expenses from his earnings. Another native son was Dr. Thomas Stewart, perhaps America's first eighteenth-century free black physician and plantation owner.

By 1850, the average value of lands by the assessment was $3.70 per acre. The county's products were mainly tobacco, lumber, cotton and wheat. While its population was a mere 4,277 whites, with 563 over the age of twenty who could not read and write, there were 6,149 slaves and 680 free blacks, of whom several—including slaves—owned property. The focus on general education started to became important for the overall economic development of this county. Similarly, the focus on occupations other than farming started to develop, while the nation's political structure again came into question.

Farming in this period seems to have been accompanied by the consolidation and final settlement of most arable areas. Agriculture remained the mainstay of the regional economy during this period. The principal crops in the region at large were tobacco, corn and, increasingly, wheat. Years of cultivation in the region rendered some farms less productive as the soil was depleted. Very large plantations in fertile sections continued to contrast with many small mixed-crop farms in other areas. The agricultural buildings that served the farmers of the period probably did not survive, although some of the outbuildings surveyed may predate 1831. These consisted principally of stables, barns, meat houses, granaries and cribs. Most of the historic farms mentioned under the domestic theme above survived to form the backbone of the county's historic agricultural landscape.

A few stores were operated to make goods and credit available to residents within the county. However, stores of this period were few, and any locations have not been identified in the secondary literature. Petersburg served as the commercial hub for the county, as well as for the region.

On March 23, 1861, James Boisseau, a delegate for Dinwiddie County at the Virginia State Convention, said, "I will state, sir—that at the time of the election, there was a very large majority in the county of Dinwiddie against secession." Mr. Boisseau corrected his earlier statement in the proceedings of March 25:

> *I may say now that the county is now almost unanimous in favor of secession. The people of my county have sons, brothers, relations and friends in the Confederated States South—persons who have left us in the pursuit of their fortunes, and who have been taken by the hand by the people of the South. They have amassed wealth, and achieved honor and distinction among the people with whom their lot has been cast; and the people of Dinwiddie will never consent to be placed in any attitude of hostility to them. Their sympathies are with those whom they regard as their friends, and they have no sympathies with those whom they regard as their enemies. I move that the proceedings be referred to the Committee on Federal Relations.*

Dinwiddie County was then only 10.5 percent slaveholder, while 42.0 percent of its total population was enslaved.

Nearly fifty engagements and battles were fought here in Dinwiddie County, including the Battle of Dinwiddie Courthouse, the Battle of Sutherland's Station and the Battle of White Oak Road, just to name a few. During the final days of the American Civil War, the Battle of Lewis's Farm was fought here on March 29, 1865, along Quaker Road (Route 660). This was the first in a series of attempts by Ulysses S. Grant's army to cut Lee's final supply line, the South Side Railroad, in spring 1865. Here, the Union forces led by Brigadier General Joshua Chamberlain engaged Confederates under Major General Bushrod R. Johnson. Chamberlain would have his horse shot out from under him at Lewis's farm on Quaker Road. After sharp fighting, the Union troops entrenched nearby along the Boydton Plank Road. Johnson withdrew to his lines at White Oak Road. The Union army cut the rail line four days later, after capturing Five Forks on April 1, 1865, at the Battle of Five Forks.

The following morning, at approximately 4:40 a.m., Lieutenant General Ulysses S. Grant sent the Sixth Corps, some 14,000 strong, pouring over the Confederate fortifications near Tudor Hall Plantation, now preserved by Pamplin Historical Park. This attack broke General Robert E. Lee's defensive line around Petersburg and compelled Lee to order the evacuation of both Petersburg and Richmond that night. Lieutenant General Ambrose P. Hill, one of Lee's highest-ranking subordinates, was killed near what is now Pamplin Historical Park while riding to take command of the battlefield. Many of its citizens have since participated in the defense of the United States of America, a proud tradition of military service that continues to this day. On April 2, only 350 Confederates held Fort Gregg, which some now call the "Confederate Alamo," against 15,000 Union troops until fewer than 50 remained, most badly wounded. Among those few left staying was a sixteen-year-old soldier from Dinwiddie County, its only representative. He quickly escaped on his way to prison. The remains of Lee's army then escaped from the county to continue the fight and to surrender at Appomattox on April 9, 1865, after four years of war and over 630,000 casualties, many of whom fell here.

Dinwiddie County has grown from this era to become a very inclusive community. Its citizens have built an outstanding educational and community services system, while providing a host of soldiers and goods for both world wars and more recent conflicts. Today, the county enjoys a healthy diversity of people, as well as cultural, religious, educational and economic interests. Small businesses have thrived, as evidenced by the county's stability. Dinwiddie's farms, service providers, manufacturing and major distribution facilities produce a wide variety of goods, having the support of two strong local community banks, the Bank of McKenney and the Southside Bank.

Throughout its history, the people of Dinwiddie have remained hardworking, industrious and friendly. They are proud of the community that they and those who came before them have created. The future holds great promise for Dinwiddie County. Its proximity to the growing edge of Virginia's "Golden Crescent" will continue to create great opportunity for its new "settlers." Dinwiddie County now includes the following unincorporated communities: Carson, Church Road, Dabney Estates, Darvills, Dewitt, village of Dinwiddie, Edgehill, Five Forks, Ford, Sutherland and Wilsons, as well as the incorporated town of McKenney.

Chapter 1

EUROPEAN SETTLEMENT TO SOCIETY

1607–1750

Dinwiddie County's first contact with the English came in May 1607, when a shallop rowed up the Appomattox River, stopping near the falls at the fault line near what would be called Petersburg. The earliest European settlement in the Dinwiddie area was at the falls of the Appomattox River, near the present site of the city of Petersburg. In the earliest days of colonial settlement on the tributaries of the James River, efforts to settle the banks of the Appomattox were thwarted by Indian hostility. An expedition in 1636 under the command of fur trader Captain Henry Fleet drove the Appomattox Indians inland and founded a fort at the falls, making settlement possible. From the falls of the Appomattox, long-established Indian trading trails, along which traveled furs and other goods, led south to Catawba, Occaneechee and Cherokee Indians; west to the Mankins; and north to the Pamunkey and Iroquois.

By 1643, Bristol Parish was established due to increasing population in the Appomattox Valley. In 1645, Fort Henry was established for the defense of the inhabitants on the south side of the James River. It was probably built partly in response to the Powhatan Indian attacks led by Opechancanough in 1622 and 1644. From 1638 to 1675, Fort Henry's commander, Abraham Wood, ascended to the rank of major general of the Virginia militia. He was active in local Indian affairs, and he revised laws of the colony and headed expeditions to the south and west. Fort Henry became a center of regional trade and western exploration. In 1675, Peter Jones succeeded Abraham Wood as leader in the area. He married Margaret Wood (Abraham's daughter), continued the trade once established by Wood, was in charge of Fort Henry and established his own trading post. Local tradition indicates that Petersburg may have been named for Peter Jones, but there is actually no supporting documentation and Petersburg, Russia, may have been a likely reference.

Reverend John Banister I (1650–1692), the rector of Bristol Parish, was an Oxford-trained botanist with a great interest in American flora. While not personally wealthy, his contacts with powerful Virginia families enabled him to greatly improve his descendants' positions. He married Martha, widow of local landowner Abraham Jones. He is now described as North America's first "resident naturalist." All his works were unpublished in his lifetime, given the lack of a Virginia printer at the time. However, the University of Illinois Press published a 485-page book, with thirty-two plates, entitled *John Banister and His Natural History of Virginia, 1678–1692,* by Joseph and Nesta Ewan, in 1970. It is described as "being a collection of his known works: a source book of plant, insect, arachnid, mollusc, and rock catalogues for the specialist; drawings, a natural history, and account of the natives for the general reader, naturalist and historian: a review of natural history literature on the New World with which he was familiar; of the persons who influenced his activities; and of the significant uses by others of his manuscripts and drawings." He appears to have been the first known owner of the valuable property along the Appomattox River west of Petersburg, which was later known as Battersea.

During Bacon's Rebellion of 1678, the Appomattox Indian village at what is now Ettrick (Chesterfield County) was burned. It would later be the boyhood home of John Randolph, of Roanoke.

Bristol Parish's first vestry was recorded on October 30, 1720, and consisted of Reverend George Robertson, Major William Kennon, Lewis Green, Major Robert Bolling, Major Robert Munford, Captain Peters Jones, Instant Hall, Captain Richard Kennon, Henry Randolph, Thomas Bott and Charles Roberts. In 1721, George Archer was named the first vestryman of Bristol Parish.

In 1730, Britain's Virginia governor was Sir William Gooch, First Baronet (October 21, 1681–December 17, 1751), a native of Great Yarmouth, Norfolk, England. Gooch's tenure as governor was characterized by his unusual political effectiveness. Gooch's successes included the passage of the Tobacco Inspection Act of 1730. This act called for the grading,

Fort Henry was a wooden fort and outpost near the Peter Jones Trading Post site at the fall line of the Appomattox River. Shown here is what remains of the trading post site. *Photo by author.*

inspection and regulation of tobacco. Planters were required to transport their tobacco to public warehouses, where it was graded, inspected, sold and stored. The act not only raised the quality of Virginia's tobacco but also reduced fraud and increased the demand for Virginia tobacco. These public warehouses would become central to the development of villages such as Petersburg and Blandford on the Appomattox River nearest to the then western frontier. These warehouses served as the cornerstone for the development of Dinwiddie County and the region, attracting merchants, artisans and mechanics to support its multicultural maritime society and supply the region's plantation system as far away as Halifax and Raleigh, North Carolina, and help further western expansion. As the next century approached, many Dinwiddians would seek out land in Ohio and Kentucky for development.

The Battersea Mill was constructed on the Appomattox River in 1732, next to the south side of an early Indian fish way. The mill would continue in operation through the American Revolution. It was not until 1733 when

Colonel William Byrd II would lead an expedition to survey newly acquired lands near the Virginia–North Carolina line. During this expedition, he laid the foundation of two towns, Richmond and Petersburg, and spent several days exploring and staying with friends in what would later be known as Dinwiddie County. William Pride's mill development began at the Appomattox's falls, after he brought the property from Major Peter Jones.

The Sappony Episcopal Church stands as an important testament to this region's pre-Revolution history. A simple frame building was first constructed in 1725–26, adjacent to a small Indian village. Reverend Devereux Jarratt served as rector there and at other congregations in Dinwiddie County from 1763 until his death in 1801. Reverend Jarratt was a prominent figure of the Anglican (later Episcopal) Church. During the Great Awakening, he preached to audiences in Southside Virginia and North Carolina and influenced the early Methodist development in this region. Reverend Jarratt was an influential Dinwiddie plantation and slave owner. In 1869, the Sappony Episcopal Church roof collapsed, and in its rebuilding, the congregation used the original pews, wainscoting, windows and railings. The bodies of both Jarratt and his wife were moved inside the church. The church is located near McKenney in Dinwiddie County, off the McKenney Highway (Route 40) and north on Shippings Road (Route 655).

Bristol Parish built Blandford Church during 1734–37. Blandford Church was later abandoned at the turn of the century and then used as a field hospital during the Civil War. The Ladies Memorial Association (LMA) began reinterring Confederate soldiers from surrounding area battlefields into Blandford Cemetery in 1866, and restoration of the church began in 1901. The LMA unveiled the various Tiffany windows between 1904 and 1912.

Quakers began settling the region by the mid-seventeenth century. Edward Staber, a Quaker druggist, purchased a twelve-acre tract west of the new town of Petersburg in what would become Dinwiddie County in 1757. There the Quakers built a meetinghouse, which they named for nearby Gravelly Run stream; the meetinghouse was built by 1767 and called the Gravelly Run Quaker Meeting House. It became the religious center for the Quakers in Dinwiddie and the surrounding counties. In the early 1800s, the "Upper Monthly Meeting" was frequently held at Gravelly Run. From this meetinghouse, Benjamin Bates presented and signed the Memorial and Petition of the Society of Friends, or Quakers, to the Legislature of Virginia on the Subject of Militia Fines, on November 17, 1810, maintaining that military service was a free exercise of conscience. This petition would be

The 1728 Anglican Church suffered a precipitous decline after the Revolution. Sappony Church appears to have been the only Anglican church in the county during the years after the Revolution. It was located near the lower end of the parish, on Sappony Creek. The entire Anglican connection with the state was abolished, and the newly renamed Episcopal Church suffered greatly from disestablishment. *Courtesy of the Library of Congress.*

The grandest manifestation of the center-passage-plan form standing today from this period is Evergreen, located north of Dinwiddie Courthouse. It is a much-altered, large, frame, two-story, five-bay, single-pile house dating from 1790 to 1810. It was originally the Butler home; the Butlers were Quakers and principals of the nearby Quaker meetinghouse, which no longer stands, and its long-forgotten cemetery, which included the elder Stablers' family graves. *Photo by author.*

reprinted several times during the War of 1812. Membership began to decline because the Quakers refused to bear arms, especially during the War of 1812, and because of their open opposition to slavery. As a result, several members moved to Ohio, Tennessee and Indiana, and the meetinghouse was abandoned in the 1830s. The location of this site is just to the east after you go over the I-85 overpass on Quaker Road, Route 660 from U.S. Route 1. Edward Staber was buried there. Nearby, the Butler families were among the earliest Quakers of Dinwiddie County. James Butler was the earliest settler, followed by Joseph Butler, who was the last Butler to maintain the 150-acre plantation known as Evergreen, now the private home of R.M. Richie on U.S. Route 1.

Chapter 2

COLONY TO NATION

1751–1789

On July 16, 1751, the *London Gazette* announced, "The King has been pleased to constitute and appoint Robert Dinwiddie, Esq., to be Lieutenant Governor of his Majesty's Colony and Dominion of Virginia in America in the Room of Sir William Gooch, Bart." Dinwiddie County was formed May 1, 1752, from Prince George County. The county is named for Robert Dinwiddie, the British lieutenant governor of colonial Virginia from 1751 to 1758, first under Governor Willem Anne van Keppel, second earl of Albemarle, and then from July 1756 to January 1758, as deputy for John Campbell, fourth earl of Loudoun. The governors at that time were largely absent, and Campbell was a de-facto head of the colony for much of this time. On July 23, 1754, the *London Gazette* announced that "the New Ship DINWIDDIE, a prime Sailor, squire stern'd, Boston built, burthen 200 tons, more or less with exceeding good dimensions for the Virginia or West India Trades, now lying at Wapping Old Stairs, Patrick Young, Commander. Inventories to be had on Board, at the place of sale, and of John Hutchinson, broker, in Exchange Alley."

Dinwiddie's actions as lieutenant governor are commonly cited as precipitating the French and Indian War. He wanted to limit French expansion in the Ohio Country, an area claimed by the Virginia Colony and in which the Ohio Company, of which he was a stockholder, had made initial surveys and some small settlements.

Under Lieutenant Governor Dinwiddie, Virginia was divided in 1752 into four military districts, each with its own officer. The troops of Dinwiddie

Robert Dinwiddie. *Author's collection.*

County, which fell in the Southern District, were commanded at first by George Washington. There was reason indeed to strengthen defenses and military organizations: France, seeking to gain possession of the West and Northwest of this newly forming territory, which belonged to Virginia by the royal charter granted to the London Company in 1609, was planning a line of forts to extend from the Great Lakes to the Spanish Floridas. Without fortifications on the Virginia frontiers, settlers in the western part of the colony were not safe, and additional lands would certainly not be patented. Having obtained permission from the Indians to erect a fort at the confluence of the Monongahela and Allegheny Rivers, Dinwiddie in 1753 appointed the twenty-one-year-old George Washington to acquaint the French with his plans. The young man delivered the warning message that paved the way for the French and Indian War, in which he was to achieve his first fame and the military preparation that enabled him to later command the American forces during the Revolution. By the deaths first of Colonel Joshua Fry and then of the British general Edward Braddock, Washington succeeded to the command of two important expeditions.

In 1753, Lord Dinwiddie learned the French had built Fort Presque Isle near Lake Erie, which he saw as a threat to Virginia's various interests in the newly discovered Ohio Valley. Dinwiddie sent an eight-man expedition under George Washington's command starting out from Williamsburg to warn the French to withdraw. Washington made the journey that winter and arrived at the French Fort Le Boeuf, near Lake Erie, on December 11, 1753. Jacques Legardeur de Saint-Pierre, commandant of the fort, received Washington politely but rejected his warning.

Washington spent three days at the fort and was given a letter to deliver to Lord Dinwiddie. The letter ordered the governor of Virginia to deliver his demand to the major general of New France in the capital, Quebec City.

In January 1754, before learning of the French refusal, Lord Dinwiddie sent a small force of Virginia militia to build a fort at the forks of the Ohio River, where the Allegheny and Monongahela Rivers merge to form the Ohio. The French quickly drove off the Virginians and built a larger fort on the site, calling it Fort Duquesne, in honor of the Marquis de Duquesne, the governor of New France.

In early spring 1754, Lord Dinwiddie sent Washington to build a road to the Monongahela and then to help defend the British fort. Learning that the French had taken the fort, Washington pressed on and built a small stockade, Fort Necessity. Here he fought the French in a skirmish on July 3, 1754, and was forced to surrender. Lord Dinwiddie rallied other colonies in defense against the French and prevailed upon the British Crown to send General Edward Braddock to Virginia with two regiments of British regular troops.

Dinwiddie County unquestionably furnished its share of volunteers to accompany Washington. One of them was Peter Brown, who suffered a mishap just as serious as a wound inflicted by an enemy but far less glamorous. He enlisted as a soldier in the expedition to the Ohio, but while he was boarding a transport at Blandford on his way to join other soldiers at Fredericksburg, "the fall of a tree" broke "both his legs and one of his thighs." His captain sent him to the home of Walter Boyd, "where he lay more than a year unable to stir without assistance." On April 9, 1756, Boyd, exclaiming that he had been at great expense and trouble and had "not yet received any satisfaction for the same," petitioned the House of Burgesses for payment. Boyd was allowed £6.1.2 for his year's work, but Peter Brown, though the committee of the House reported that he had been rendered "utterly incapable of getting a livelihood," was given a mere £6. Peter Brown was only a humble soldier, overtaken by a calamity that caused his name to survive in the records. Arthur Watts of Dinwiddie, however, served George Washington well during the Northwest campaign and later was made a member of the county's committee of safety. In January 1758, Dinwiddie left Virginia and lived in England until his death at Clifton, Bristol. It's unlikely Lord Dinwiddie ever visited the county named after him.

The early Dinwiddie County population was starting to expand, and as the number of families continued to rise through the mid-1700s, a new generation of Virginia-born youth characterized this era. Meanwhile, England was reeling in profits from the Navigation Acts. By the 1740s, a current of English goods began to gush into the colonies, revealing a transatlantic empire that was driven by consumer demand. British entrepreneurs such as Josiah Wedgewood catered to this demand and first created the standards of dress and household display that the English (and later Virginia aristocrats) adopted, and the classes below them could afford to emulate. Never before had such a consumer boom taken place; this was a society where even the lowest landowning farmer could afford to spend beyond bounds of practicality, with goods advertised in London newspapers and displayed in the storefront windows of Williamsburg, where Virginia capitalism was born. America was driven by the middle class, and Williamsburg had certainly become a consumer hub for a new breed of middle-class shoppers. The age of consumption was important firstly because it showed the evolving Virginian society, one in which its people, from rich to poor, had become economically established enough to purchase differentiated goods. Secondly, it revealed the interdependence between the colonies and England during this time, a dependence that wayward colonists would desire to break free from in just a few years.

Women played a crucial role in cidering and general distilling in colonial Dinwiddie. Cider was essential to colonial life; the Dinwiddie's water was generally foul, there were only a few deep wells and tea and coffee were too expensive for most. Colonists used some form of alcohol to drink, in cooking and sometimes as medicine.

The county is historically defined by the series of creeks flowing south into the Nottoway River and north into the Appomattox River. The watercourses define the geography of Dinwiddie County. The Appomattox River's bottomlands and the higher ground overlooking them were the sites of a series of great plantations and grand houses in the mid- to late eighteenth century. Dinwiddie County has been the home of many farms and plantations within its five hundred square miles.

The next important historic location elements in the county were the three principal roads extending from the trading hub of Petersburg in the northeastern corner of Dinwiddie County. The Halifax Road runs south along the eastern edge of the county all the way to Halifax, North

John Banister. *Author's collection.*

Carolina. Cocke's (Cox) Road runs west, parallel to the Appomattox River and Namozine Creek. Boydton Plank Road (Historic U.S. Route 1) runs southwest across the center of the county and through the county seat at Dinwiddie. Minor roads tend to cross the county from the northwest to southeast and are aligned with river crossings and the county seat.

The original first settlements were often located near prominent river crossings, including the first courthouse and the nearby county seat of later date. The earliest churches were Anglican, Quaker and Baptist and generally helped to define three principal sections in the county. They were named for prominent creeks: Hatcher's Run and Gravelly Creek in the center, Butterwood in the west and Sappony to the south referred to the churches and the three principal sections of the county.

Howell Briggs (1709–1775) came to the county prior to the French and Indian War and was made famous by his posterity. As a very young man, he had come to the future Dinwiddie and, with his bride, had established his home at a place he named Wales in honor of the crown prince of England. In 1754, his son, Gray Briggs, became one of the first burgesses from Sussex County.

John Banister III, a delegate from Virginia, was born at Hatcher's Run, near Petersburg, in Dinwiddie County, on December 26, 1734. He attended a private school at Wakefield, England, and graduated in law from the Temple, which is one of the main legal districts and a notable center for English law, both historically and in the present day, in London. He returned to Virginia and commenced the practice of law in Petersburg. He was also engaged as a planter in Dinwiddie while he served as a member of the Virginia House of Burgesses from 1765 to 1775. During the Revolutionary War, Banister served as major and lieutenant colonel of the Virginia Militia. He served in the state house of delegates in 1776, 1777 and from 1781 to 1783. He was a member of the Continental Congress in 1778 and served as one of the framers and signers of the Articles of Confederation.

Battersea, located some miles away to the north, was built in 1768 for Colonel John Banister and has been called, in spite of extensive Federal-style alterations, "one of the earliest and finest surviving examples of a five-part, Robert Morris–style Palladian house in the United States," a design derived from the architectural publications of Andrea Palladio and Robert Morris. Battersea was a second home intended to serve as a suburban villa near Banister's urban and industrial interests in Petersburg.

John Banister died on his primary estate, Hatcher's Run, on September 30, 1788, and was buried in the family cemetery there.

THE AMERICAN REVOLUTION

Local Committees of Correspondence were substitute governments organized by the Patriot leaders of the thirteen colonies on the eve of the Revolution; the Loyalists were, of course, excluded. By 1773, these committees had emerged as local independent governments, superseding the colonial legislature and royal officials. They directed responses to Britain and shared their plans with each other, examined merchant records and published the names of those who attempted to defy the boycott by importing British goods. They promoted patriotism, home manufacturing, avoiding luxuries and leading a simpler life. Committees of Safety were in constant communication with Committees of Correspondence, which disseminated information among the militia units and provided a clearinghouse of information and intelligence on enemy activities. Local militias were usually under their control.

Increasing political and military tensions in early 1775 caused both Lord Dunmore and rebellious Whig leaders to recruit troops and engage in a struggle for available military supplies. That struggle eventually focused on Norfolk, where Dunmore had taken refuge aboard a Royal Navy vessel. Dunmore's forces had fortified one side of a critical river crossing south of Norfolk at Great Bridge, while Whig forces had occupied the other side. In an attempt to break up the Whig gathering, Dunmore ordered an attack across the bridge, which was decisively repulsed. William Woodford, the Whig commander at the battle, described it as "a second Bunker's Hill affair." Shortly thereafter, Norfolk, at the time a Tory center, was abandoned by Dunmore, and many of the Norfolk Tories fled to navy ships. Norfolk was later destroyed on January 1, 1776, in an action begun by Dunmore and completed by the Whig forces. Peterson Goodwyn would die on February 21, 1818, and is buried in the Goodwyn Family Cemetery in Dinwiddie County.

The following ad in the *Virginia Gazette* is likely what prompted James Geddy II, a noted silversmith, and his young family to leave behind their home in Williamsburg. That home still stands near the former British Governor's Palace, Lord Dunmore's home, in Colonial Williamsburg.

> *For Sale*
> *A tract of land, containing 444 acres, in the county of Dinwiddie, on the Nottoway River, near the Lew Jones bridge, and within 35 miles of Petersburg. The land is good for tobacco and all kinds of grain, there are about 150 acres of choice low grounds, a charming apple orchard, and a tolerable dwelling-house 28' by 26', together with kitchen, dairy, smoke-house, & c. For terms apply to the subscriber, on the premises.*
> *John Corryton.*

The Geddy family stayed along the Nottoway River for the duration of the war and then moved into the town of Petersburg. There is no visible trace of their plantation, and the deed records have been lost.

Early colonial Dinwiddie was home to several other artisans besides the Geddys. William and Noel Waddill were also both silversmiths and apparent associates of the Geddys; Andrew, John and Stith Hardway were gunsmiths; Matthew Mayes was a blacksmith and gunsmith; David Fisher and Robert McKeen were cabinetmakers; James Williams was a blacksmith and bell founder; and Abner Adams, Joseph Haxall, Robert Reames, James Howard, John Scott Coleman, Charles Williamson, Frederick Jones and David Walker were all carpenters.

By 1775, Dinwiddie County had already begun to prepare for the pending conflict. On June 10, 1775, the "Volunteer Company of Dinwiddie County" had advertised in the *Virginia Gazette* that it "would willingly engage with an expert Adjutant to instruct them in military Discipline." The county Committee of Correspondence was soon serious about the business of running down people suspected of giving information to the enemy. Thomas Irving served as deputy postmaster and was carefully watched.

By early June 1775, the Committee of Correspondence focused on "the conduct of Messr. Eilbeck & Ross, and that they would prevent any of the[ir] goods from being loaded or disposed of within their counties." Eilbeck, Ross and company were well-established British merchants operating on the wharfs of Petersburg.

On November 15, 1775 the Dinwiddie Committee of Correspondence "resolved that no provisions of any kind, or fuel, be here after allowed to be carried from this county, by land or water, without a permit from the Honorable Committee of Safety or the Committee of this county." This notice wasn't published until December 29, 1775, in Williamsburg's *Virginia Gazette*, a month and a half after the event, an indication how fast war news traveled within Virginia at this time.

Militia men from Dinwiddie County would enlist through the Southampton County recruiting district, which included Sussex, Surry, Brunswick and Prince George Counties. Captain Edwards, of Dinwiddie, helped lead some of these men. The battalion commander was Colonel David Mason, assisted by Lieutenant Colonel John Ruffin. Dinwiddie's Committee of Safety helped to oversee their needs. This committee was elected November 20, 1775, and was made up of twenty-one county civilians, with John Jones serving as clerk.

On January 2, 1776, the Dinwiddie Committee of Correspondence addressed the following letter to Edmund Pendleton, president of the Virginia Convention:

> *Hon'ble Sir:*
>
> *The committee of correspondence for Dinwiddie County begs leave to inform you that a certain Thomas Irving an inhabitant of this town is deputy post-master for Mr. Dixon that he is also an agent for Neil Jameison, who we understand is inimical to this country, and a partisan of Lord Dunmore's. The committee would not chuse to be officious in acting without authority from the Convention, but are clearly of opinion it is highly improper and may be of great prejudice to suffer the said Irving to continue post-master which may give him an opportunity by opening letters—of conveying intelligence of the most dangerous nature to the welfare of this Colony.*

> *We are fully persuaded that in no other part of America would an agent for an avowed enemy, at this time assisting Lord Dunmore in the most atrocious acts of violence and despotism be suffered to keep open store in the heart of that very country on which they are using every diabolical measure in their power to bring ruin and desolation. Tho' solicitous to serve our country ever ready to offer the right hand of friendship in the cause of Liberty, yet we are anxious not to exceed the line of our duty and therefore beg, Sir, you would be pleased to point it out to us.*
>
> *We are Your Honours most obed't and very humble Servants, William Harrison, Bolling Starke, and Joseph Jones.*

During the American Revolution, the counterfeiter Benjamin Woodward furnished the people of Dinwiddie with excitement and the state with considerable expense. He was the leader of a gang that printed excellent copies of the new paper currency of Virginia and neighboring states. Woodward was arrested in the summer of 1776 and taken to the Dinwiddie courthouse, where he was to appear "before John Banister Esquire or any other magistrate of the said County and dealt with according to law." Shem Cook, Joseph Cook, Frederick Ray and Joseph Ray, suspected of being Woodward's accomplices, were also arrested and sent to Pittsylvania County, where they claimed a right to be tried. Woodward and a bag of his implements were delivered to jail. Woodward was examined by the Court of Dinwiddie County and "remanded to Jail in order to take his trial," but he escaped. A reward of $650 was offered "to any person who shall apprehend the said Woodward and deliver him to the Keeper of the Public Jail."

It was discovered that the counterfeiter had many accomplices in his scheme to defraud the government. In December 1778, while Benjamin Woodward was still at large, the governor received under oath a list naming twenty-one men who were also implicated. The less important members of the ring were arrested. The law required the death penalty; the lives of four were spared, according to a statement made in 1782 by William Rose, the jailor, "provided they performed three years' Service each, as Common Laborers in the public lead mines."

In 1784, Virginia strengthened its law concerning the treatment of counterfeiters by imposing "death without benefit of clergy, that is, capital punishment with no chance to obtain divine forgiveness, upon makers of counterfeit money and those persons handling the money and knowing the same to be forged." In 1790, James Arthur, having been arrested on the charge of counterfeiting, made a confession revealing Benjamin Woodward to be the brains of the criminal gang. James Wood, lieutenant governor of Virginia, issued a proclamation for Woodward's arrest and offered $150 for his "apprehension & conveyance…to the District jail of Petersburg."

John and Tinsley Young discovered more of the implements in Dinwiddie County with which Woodward printed the certificates, including several thousand pounds in counterfeit North Carolina bills, as well as tools for counterfeiting and coining. The Young brothers only received a reward of seven pounds through the efforts of Robert Bolling and Goodwyn. The news of this discovery must have electrified the people of Dinwiddie, and the recently discovered implements and the confession of James Arthur were quite enough to convict Woodward. Arthur's statement indicated, moreover, that Benjamin Woodward, during the years he was a fugitive from justice, had been in Virginia, plying his trade as a maker of paper certificates and coins, and that through agents in Virginia and many other states, he had done a profitable business. The following "gentlemen justices" were present at the examination of Arthur: James Greenway, Edward Pegram Jr., William Watts, Raleigh Downman, Joseph Whitehead, Francis Meier, Frederick Jones, Joseph Turner, Peterson Goodwyn, Wood Tucker, Jordan Reese and Henry Spain. According to Arthur's confession, Woodward had been operating in Petersburg, Richmond, Portsmouth and Norfolk, using other men to "pass" the certificates and coin of his making. He, along with "his negro fellow," James Arthur, and others, struck off the certificates. Many of these Arthur confessed to having signed, as Woodward cleverly hid behind his accomplices. Woodward had often use the surname of Jones, but he would become so intoxicated that he would often call out, "Here is Ben Woodward, the money maker." Arthur's testimony showed that agents active in Richmond, Norfolk, Maryland and North Carolina had prospered. Gold dust for the coins was hidden in trunks and conveyed from place to place. Paper for the certificates came from a mill in Maryland via Jesse Woodward, Benjamin's brother.

Benjamin Woodward was finally caught in Augusta, Georgia. On October 12, 1791, Governor Beverley Randolph sent to William Rose, the jailor, the following letter, which must have excited all the law-abiding citizens of Dinwiddie County:

> *Sir, Mr. Longstreet with a guard, who have in custody Benjamin Woodward, who is taken up under a proclamation of the State, intend to lodge at your*

> *house this night. Their necessary expenses will be paid by the Executive. You will be good enough to provide for them the most secure room in your house, as the Culprit cannot be regularly committed to GOAL in this county.*
> *I am, Sir, Your Ob't Serv't. Beverley Randolph*

Woodward's identity had been established by Robert Dixon, William Nicholson and George Poythress, who knew him well and had traveled all the way to Augusta to look him over. Though fifteen years had passed since Woodward escaped from jail in Dinwiddie, the three men recognized him and testified under oath that he was "the identical person who was formerly a resident of Dinwiddie County, in the State of Virginia, and has long been noted for his villainy for counterfeiting the public papers of that State."

As soon as Richard Bate, the then mayor of Petersburg, heard that Benjamin Woodward had been caught, he requested "any person that can give evidence either for or against the said Woodward, touching the said offence" to be ready to attend the examination. Woodward was taken from Augusta, Georgia, to Charleston, South Carolina, and then was brought to Richmond, where he arrived under guard on October 12, 1791. He was sent the next day to Dinwiddie in the custody of Richard Zourtney and Larkin Philips. Incomplete records somewhat obscure Benjamin Woodward's career. He escaped a second time from Dinwiddie in 1795; he can be traced to Maryland, where he was arrested for stealing horses and identified as the notorious Virginia counterfeiter, though he had adopted the good old Dinwiddie name of Peter Jones. The man was undoubtedly clever, for Edward and John Pegram, sent from Dinwiddie in 1795 to bring back the fugitive, returned without him. It can only be hoped that Benjamin Woodward at last received the extreme penalty for his major crime, "death without benefit of clergy."

On April 24, 1781, British forces landed at City Point and commenced to march on Petersburg. A few traveled upriver on flatboats equipped with small artillery pieces. The next day, the Battle of Petersburg saw 2,500 British soldiers under Major General William Phillips and a forced march of 1,000 militia under Major General Baron Von Steuben in retreat across the Appomattox River. General William Phillips would die on May 13 at Bollingbrook and was secretly buried somewhere in Blandford Cemetery. This was a full-blown battle by Revolutionary War standards, involving 3,500 men engaged for upward of three hours. On April 26, British major general William Phillips had his troops burn all the ships in the Petersburg harbor. Boyd's warehouses, run by Christopher McConnico, full of tobacco were also removed and burned, all to the alarm and hardship of the civilian inhabitants of this county.

Though the fighting of the Revolution was focused for the first years in the North, far South and Northwest, Virginia furnished provisions, leaders and companies of soldiers and strove at the same time to strengthen home defenses. Prominent among the men who were engaged in Revolutionary activities were Lieutenant Colonel Francis Eppes, John Banister, Captain Edward Walker and Richard Taylor.

Richard Taylor had much to do with supplying provisions for the soldiers of the Revolution. His home was Spring Garden, actually in Prince George County but very near Petersburg. His son by the same name, however, lived within the town. Another son, George Keith Taylor, has been called the father of penal reform in Virginia, but more on him later. The elder Richard Taylor was a merchant and the owner of a mill. Shortly before the Revolution, Roger Atkinson, of Mansfield in Dinwiddie County, wrote that "Dick Taylor is erecting and hath begun a fine Merc't mill…Dick will be rich and I think he deserves it."

So the council resolved on June 7, 1776, that this successful merchant should "be employed to furnished [*sic*] the minutemen ordered to Rendezvous at Petersburg, with provisions while they remain at that place." These minutemen served as patrols along the James River. Vessels came to the town for arms and provisions or to seek a place of safety.

Though British general Sir Banastre Tarleton failed to capture Virginia governor Thomas Jefferson, first at Richmond and then at Monticello, General Benedict Arnold, having reached Virginia, pillaged his way up the James and reached Petersburg. Despite the valiant resistance of General Von Steuben and General Muhlenburg, he created much havoc and destroyed the stores on which the American army depended. British major general William Phillips arrived with more troops and provisions and established his headquarters in Petersburg at Bollingbrook, the home of the late Robert Bolling and his widow. Bolling had settled at Bollingbrook, and in 1765, 1768 and 1770, he represented Dinwiddie County in the House of Burgesses. Bollingbrook stood on the East Hill overlooking the Appomattox; a little upriver, Bolling also once operated one of the earliest known mills on the Dinwiddie side. Mrs. Robert Bolling was imprisoned in the east wing of her house in a back room. In the yard were two sentries, who stood guard with crossed bayonets. The British set fire to the fences about Bollingbrook.

General Phillips became ill at the Robert Bolling home. Soon after Lafayette cannonaded the town, Phillips breathed his last, exclaiming in despair that the Americans would not even let him die in peace. General Arnold then assumed command of the British forces in Virginia but was relieved by General Cornwallis, who marched through Dinwiddie, probably along the Stage and Halifax Roads, and reached Petersburg soon thereafter. So it happened that from Dinwiddie County the British set out for Yorktown and for the defeat that led to the permanent establishment of these United States of America. Thus it came about that the county figured prominently toward the end of this war and of another war, more tragic, that resulted in cementing the Union.

The war brought new financial difficulties. The Continental Congress was powerless to impose taxes and thus was forced to print massive amounts of currency to help finance the war. This caused Continental currency to rapidly depreciate; by 1781, the paper was exchangeable for coin at a ratio of 225 to 1 ($225 in paper for a $1 coin).

Thomas Stewart was born about 1727. He was a medical doctor in Dinwiddie County, and on November 13, 1778, the following notice appeared in the *Virginia Gazette*:

> *I Nathaniel Hobbs, of Dinwiddie County, do hereby certify, that in the month of May last my Negro boy Tom received a kick from a stallion in the forehead, which deprived him of his senses from Sunday until Tuesday evening in which time he lost a quantity of blood, and many ounces of matter, supposed to be part of his brain, but by the assistance of Dr. Thomas Stewart, of Dinwiddie, and his specific balsam, he is now perfectly well, and as sound and sensible as ever.*

What this paid notice by Nathaniel Hobbs doesn't tell you is that Nathaniel was then a white overseer on a nearby plantation in Dinwiddie County, and Dr. Thomas Stewart was a respected free black resident of Dinwiddie County. Dr. Stewart was a free tithable (subject or liable to payment of tithes/tax) in the county, with seventeen slaves and 874 acres in 1782. The land tax records of Mecklenburg County, Virginia, list a grant of 362 acres to Thomas Stewart. He was taxed on 720 additional acres in Mecklenburg County from 1782 to 1793. Dr. Thomas Stewart was taxable in Dinwiddie County on 874 acres on Walker's Road from 1787 to 1789 and on 845 acres from 1790 to 1807. The February 1789 session of the Dinwiddie County court granted him permission to keep an ordinary in his house. Between

Elizabeth Keckley. *Author's collection.*

March 1789 and March 1790, he sued four persons for debt in Dinwiddie County court, and it was an unusual occurrence for a black man to be allowed into court. While a resident in Dinwiddie County, he was taxed in Mecklenburg County on slaves Berry, Patty and Lewis in 1787; taxed on Frederick Gowen (a relation) and slaves Berry, Judy, Patty and Lewis in 1788; taxed on his son Charles and four slaves in 1790; taxed on his sons Charles and Joseph and four slaves in 1791; and taxed on son Joseph and five slaves in 1793. On December 5, 1792, he made a gift to his son James Stewart of 150 acres in Mecklenburg County, adjoining the land of his brother, James Stewart. His grandson John Day described him as "a coloured man of Dinwiddie County, Virginia whose name was Thomas Stewart, a medical doctor."

U.S. congressman and Revolutionary War officer Peterson Goodwyn, a Virginia Republican, was elected to eight consecutive terms in the U.S. House of Representatives, serving from 1803 until his death on February 21, 1818. Goodwyn was born at the Martins' estate near Petersburg, Virginia, into a family of planters. He was primarily home-schooled. At the start of the Revolution, he equipped his own company and was promoted to colonel for gallantry at the Battle of Great Bridge on December 9, 1775. The victory by the Continental army and militia forces led to the departure of Governor Lord Dunmore and any remaining vestiges of British power from the colony of Virginia.

Elizabeth Keckley was born a slave in February 1818 in Dinwiddie County, just five miles south of the courthouse. Her mother, Agnes, was a slave owned by Armistead and Mary Burwell. "Aggy" (Elizabeth's mother), as she was called, was considered a privileged slave, learning to read and write despite the fact that it was illegal for slaves to do so. Elizabeth's biological father, whose real identity was revealed to her later in life, was Armistead Burwell, her mother's white master and a plantation owner. In fact, Elizabeth didn't find out that Armistead Burwell was her father until her mother was on her deathbed and announced it to her. Agnes was later permitted to marry George Pleasant Hobbs. George Hobbs was also a literate slave, residing at the home of a neighbor during Elizabeth's early childhood. Hobbs was eventually estranged from his wife and stepdaughter when his owner moved far away. Elizabeth resided in the Burwell house with her mother and began official duties at age five, when it was decided that because the Burwells had four other children under the age of ten, she would become the nursemaid for their infant daughter, Elizabeth Margaret. Taking on this responsibility as a young child, she also came to understand the dynamics of a slave's existence early in her life. While looking after the baby one day, she accidentally tipped the cradle over too far, and the infant rolled onto the floor. This resulted in the beginning of many painful episodes of abuse that Elizabeth had to endure. She would go on to raise a son only to see him killed fighting in the Union army during the Civil War. At this same time, she labored as Mrs. Abraham Lincoln's seamstress as a free person, having earlier bought her own freedom. She later published her diaries about that period in her life and received criticism from Mrs. Lincoln for her candor. She died in Washington, D.C., in May 1907.

From the pen of John Banister, there survives an account of those days in Petersburg that preceded the surrender at Yorktown. The following letter was written to his friend Mr. Bland.

> *Richmond, 16th May, 1781*
> *My Dear Sir:*
> *Notwithstanding I have written four letters to you, since I have had the pleasure of one from you, I cannot forbear to acquaint you of the late very distressing scenes that have taken place, at and near Petersburg. We were not, as I wrote you, visited by Arnold, in his first expedition into the country, but General Phillips, coming to Portsmouth with reinforcement, enabled them to come up the river, with about 2,500, at a time when the militia were all discharged to about 1000. On Wednesday, the 24th, they approached Petersburg, by the way of my White-Hall plantation, where they halted in the heat of the day, and refreshed; then proceeded at about two o'clock, to advance in two columns—one by the old road, leading to the church, the other along the lane and across the ravine at Miller's old mill; here they received a fire from Captain House of Burnswick County, at the head of forty militia, which was supposed to do execution, but only a Jauger was known by us to have been killed. Captain House continued to retreat and fire, until he came to Taylor's mill, where he joined Colonel Dick, at the head of 300 picked militia, who kept up a constant fire, and prevented there, taking the heights for upwards of half an hour, but attaining these, they, with cannon and three times the force, dislodged Dick from his ground, but, notwithstanding, he made a regular and steady retreat through Blandford, and formed behind a battalion posted at Bollingbrook warehouses, their right extending to Mrs. Bolling's gate, their left to the warehouse, their front the morass, opposite to the warehouse, terminating at Blandford bridge, which Dick had taken up as his infantry crossed. This was our last resistance. The enemy advanced*

in front, their infantry and German Riflemen; against these, our battalion kept up a steady and constant fire, until they were ordered to retreat, which was not until four pieces of cannon from the hill, between Dr. Black's and Mrs. Bolling's, flanked them effectually; they then retreated in order, along the causeway, by the river to Pocahontas bridge, which they took up, but ascending the hill to gain the Heights, by T. Shore's house, the enemy played their cannon with such skill, that they killed and wounded ten of our men.

All of the wounded are since dead. Our cannon were served well from Baker's but the enemy's extreme caution has prevented our getting an account of their killed and wounded; the former though, it is clear, was not less than fourteen. The latter were sent down the river in their gun-boats. By the way, these guns-boats are of infinite use to the enemy, bringing them up in force to the shallowest landing. They carry from fifty to eighty men. After our militia had gained the hill, they retreated towards Chesterfield Courthouse, where they halted the next day. This little affair shows plainly the militia will fight, and proves that if we had force to have occupied the Heights, they would not with that force have entered the town. In consequence of this action, I was obliged to abandon my house, leaving all to the mercy of the enemy. The enemy, the next day, ordered the inhabitants to move out the tobacco, or the warehouses should be consumed with it. By the exertions of the people, the tobacco was removed, and by the soldiery burnt, and the houses spared, except Cedar-Point, which was put in flames by a soldier without order. The day after this business, the whole army crossed the Appomattox, and then after burning the bridge, proceeded to Osborne's, and having there destroyed the shipping to a great amount in value and number, shipped off the tobacco, they marched on to Manchester, where, on Richmond-hill, we remained with a superior force, (I mean to the detachment sent for this purpose) quiet spectators of the destruction of all the warehouses and tobacco, with several dwelling houses adjoining. They marched that evening to Osborne's and on Tuesday, the 31st, they embarked at the Hundred, and sailed down the river, as far as Burwell's, where upon the arrival of an advice-boat, they all stood up the river, and arrived in the night of last Thursday, again in Petersburg, and I was again obliged to retreat, leaving them in possession of all my estate. They have not as yet burned my mills, but have taken all the bread and flour, to the amount of £800, or £100-eleven of my best Negroes the first time, and now I expect they will get the rest. Your man I sent to Amelia I believe he is yet safe.

Your father received the following protection from General Phillips:
It is Major General Phillips' positive orders, that no part of the property of Colonel Theodorick Bland, receive any injury from his Majesty's Troops.

J. W. NOBLE, Aid de Camp, Major G. Phillips.
April 25th, 1781

Major General Phillips is very happy to show this favor, on account of Colonel Bland Junior's many civilities to the troops of convention, at Charlottesville.

The troops still continue at Petersburg, and expect Lord Cornwallis from Halifax [North Carolina], *where the van of his army, under Tarleton, is arrived. It is very clear, without naval aid the enemy will be possessed of the lower country, as the people are tired of the war, and come to the field most reluctantly. This, added to our exhausted finances, and bad councils, with a powerful enemy in the country, are prognostics of no favorable complexion. In my last, I touched largely upon the conduct of Eastern friends, in this day of peril, compared with our conduct to them, in their day of trial. Greene is in South Carolina, but how employed, we are not informed. Before you receive this, it is probable the enemy will have penetrated to Fredericksburg, and have destroyed all the tobacco in their route. I beg to hear if we are to expect any assistance from the eastern confederates, or our allies. If you write, George Nicholson, who is in Philadelphia, will give a ready conveyance to the letter. Jack, who is the only one of my family with me, joins in affectionate regards to Mrs. Bland, and Bob, with your sincere friend, John Banister.*

Forged slave passes and certificates of freedom have been discovered within the county. An extract of a letter from Petersburg, dated August 19, 1785, and published in the *Pennsylvania Packet and Daily Advertiser* on September 7, states:

Some days ago it was discovered that a person unknown in this town was selling out Certificates of Freedom and Passes to the Slaves, and forging such people's names as were most likely to answer the purpose. By the activity and vigilance of some gentlemen in town, this dangerous villain was apprehended last night, about ten o'clock, in company with some slaves, and just as he had finished a pass for one of them. He was carried before a Magistrate, who committed him to prison for further trial. He at first called himself Joe Thompson, but says his name is Thompson Davis. When he was first apprehended, he entreated one of the gentlemen to shoot him with the pistol he had in his hand, and discovered such a behavior as thoroughly indicated that he suspected some other charge against him, besides the forgeries he had committed and upon tracing his conduct during the time he has been in this place, he is rendered still more suspicious, wherefore the following description is given of him. He is a native of Ireland, about 5 feet 4 inches high, stout made, stoops a little, short dark brown hair, a deep scar on the right side of his forehead, just below his hair, the right eye is a little remarkable, having the appearance of a film on it, appears to be about 38 years of age, says he is a baker by trade, and that he came last from Richmond, where he had been some time soliciting his pay as a dragoon in Colonel Baylor's regiment.

Chapter 3

EARLY NATIONAL PERIOD

1790–1830

The earliest Dinwiddie County census records included the town of Petersburg and state that 13,934 persons resided here. The majority of the inhabitants—7,334 in 1790—were slaves.

On April 15, 1791, the president of the United States stopped for breakfast at Jesse Lees's tavern on the Old Halifax Road. George Washington described the area as "newly set up upon a small scale" while passing through the southeast corner of Dinwiddie County on his way to Halifax, North Carolina. Tradition has it that Washington stopped at the inn for breakfast, having left Petersburg some twelve miles behind and made a speech under the old pear tree there. There is no known record of what Washington may have said.

Tempe Coleman, a dark brown, "well-made woman, five feet two inches high, twenty six years old," was liberated by a judgment of the General Court of John Hardaway, of Dinwiddie County, as being a descendant of an Indian in 1794. Later, Daniel Coleman—described as a dark brown free black or Indian, six feet two inches tall, about forty-six years old, short bushy hair, a little grey—also obtained his freedom by a judgment of the General Court in November 1797, though he was formerly held as a slave by Joseph Hardaway.

Dr. James Greenway, a Dinwiddie neighbor of the Winfield Scotts, was born in England, near the border of Scotland. He had learned his father's trade, that of a weaver. He became familiar with the Greek, Latin, French and Italian languages. After his immigration to Virginia, he prepared himself for the practice of medicine and soon acquired a large and lucrative practice. He was devoted to the study of botany and left a *hortus siccus* (a collection of dried plants mounted, labeled and systematically arranged for use in scientific study) of forty folio volumes, in which he described the more interesting plants of Virginia and North Carolina. He was honored by memberships in several of the learned European societies and was a correspondent of the celebrated Swedish naturalist Carolus Linnæus. He taught music to his own children. Dr. Greenway wrote the following letter in 1794, on his treatment of the autumnal bilious fever in Dinwiddie County. It was not published until 1804 in the *Philadelphia Journal of Medicine*.

> *You ask if our Autumnal Fever is ever contagious. I answer, no, never contagious. The Blacks are not so subject to it, or too common intermittent, as the White people. Nor do they have it so bad; nor do they require more than half the medicines that White people do, when these last are sick of it.*
>
> *It arises from effluvia exhaling from mud and from water at rest, though deep, such as mill-ponds, the same exhalations are produced. I took the infection myself, some time ago, from the exhalation of stagnant water, covered with a scum, and suffered all the usual symptoms of the Bilious Remittent common to this climate.*
>
> *The autumnal fever attacked sooner, and with more violence, last fall, than it has done in the last 25 years past. It was more tediously continuing; required more medicines to cure it; the sick were more liable to relapse, and many of them still remain in a weak state. The winter has been too warm, and not sufficiently cold to brace them.*
>
> *A yellowness of the skin, but always in the eyes, takes place in every one attacked with our fall-fever; and I have, now and then, seen one very yellow. Some I have seen spurt up bile from the stomach, without any motion to vomit. But these were such as had lived in low places, for a long time; or had often exposed themselves to the inclemency of the weather.*
>
> *In the autumnal fever all suffer more or less in the stomach. There is a continual nausea, and frequently a vomiting of yellow or green bile, particularly during the exacerbation of the fever. A bilious diarrhea sometimes attends the fever towards its remission, and is generally salutary; but in sickly places, the bile is secreted in such quantity that it continually discharges through the intestines, until the patient becomes emaciated and dies.*
>
> *Costiveness is still a more common symptom, occasioned by a spasmodic stricture in the intestines caused by the heat and acrimony of the bile passing through, and out of, the ductus communis choledochus, in a vitiated state.*

> *A pain and heat about the region of the liver, and a heat and burning (as they themselves frequently express it) in the stomach, are very grievous and common complaints. A scarlet eruption, or petechiae, sometimes appears on the skin, like those caused by the stinging of nettles; and these came out regularly with the exacerbation of the fever, and totally vanished in every remission: and where the paroxysms are alternately worse, these spots only attend the worst fit, and do not appear in the milder one. Patients suffering under this eruption are all costive, and have a vomiting.*
>
> *A continual hiccup seizes on some; hot air and warm drinks increase it. An inflammation now and then falls upon the leg, with great pain and redness from the ankle to the knee; and the chilliness, fever, and all the symptoms become more moderate, and almost vanish.*
>
> *The fever is a double tertian, the paroxysms alternately worse, and alternately corresponding in the periods of their return; to-day it comes on at noon, to-morrow at night. The fever never goes quite off, but becomes more moderate, until chilliness ushers in the next, paroxysm. The worst paroxysm is ushered in by the greatest coldness, and this is followed by a fever proportionally exasperated in all its symptoms. The next paroxysm is milder, and all the symptoms, in degree, less violent. The greatest fit is, perhaps, attended with vomiting; the lesser one, perhaps, has neither chilliness nor vomiting.*
>
> *This was the appearance of our fever, last autumn; but there is one symptom I had liked to have forgotten. The piles were, in a few patients, very troublesome and painful: the hemorrhoidal veins swelled, and distended with blood, brought on inflammation and excruciating pain in the rectum, with costiveness. The danger was great, because the rectum, closed up with the turgid vessels, would not admit of injections; and laxatives taken by the mouth, produced, in their operation, great pain, and an increase of the fever and inflammation. I was, therefore, obliged to imitate nature, in her operation on the inflamed leg, before-mentioned; and this never failed of success.*
>
> *Wine, bark, and opium, were the common weapons that this disease was attacked with; and many died.*
>
> *I am an old-fashioned follower of Sydenham, and proceeded on his plan and method of cure. The consequence of it was that not a single patient of mine died, though I attended some that were very old, even of the age of sixty, and seventy; and one near eighty, who all recovered, and are still alive.*

Several families migrated westward from Dinwiddie County at this time, including that of Frederick Bonner, who was born on November 4, 1758, in Dinwiddie County. He had married Elizabeth Smith on September 28, 1779, in Dinwiddie. Frederick owned a plantation near Reams Station and was a prominent member of the Methodist Episcopal Church. In 1802, after he had made an exploratory trip to Ohio, the Bonner family and friends assembled their wagon train at Petersburg, thence traveling through the Cumberland Gap to Cincinnati, then northeast to the Little Miami River and following the Bullskin Trail. By 1803, he had settled just two miles south of Xenia in Greene County, Ohio. He had owned slaves but was reportedly very much antislavery. The supposition is that he moved to Ohio because it was a free state. This Bonner family traces its lineage back to Captain Thomas Bonner, who in 1642 immigrated to the colony of Virginia and later settled at Reams Station. He came from Kent, England, and the family was of Norman origin. He served in the Revolutionary War and was given a grant of five thousand acres of land in the Virginia Reserve of southwestern Ohio. Frederick Bonner died on March 23, 1830, at Greene County, Ohio.

John Day (1772–1854) was born in Dinwiddie County, Virginia, on April 15, 1772, about six miles south of Petersburg, Virginia, at Reams Station on the old Halifax Road, where Frederick Bonner arrived in the early 1700s. John's father may have been John Day, who resided in the village of Pocahontas, near Petersburg. The younger John apprenticed as a youth, probably with one of the early cabinetmakers of Petersburg or even perhaps with his father. On February 18, 1796, he married Martha Todd, who was born July 1, 1771, and known as Patsy. In 1798, he purchased 6 acres from Frederick Bonner, which he sold in 1803 to George Lloyd, who was then assembling a tract of 260 acres. The proceeds were doubtless used for the family's western journey to Ohio. They joined Frederick Bonner, who had been awarded 5,000 acres in Ohio for his Revolutionary War participation. The Day and Bonner party totaled fifteen members, with three blacks and four loads of equipment.

They started April 1, 1803, taking fifty-two days to make the journey. But they suffered a disaster en route at Flynn's Ford on the Ohio River; Day's light wagon was swept into the dangerous current. His wife, Patsy, and seven-year-old daughter, Susan, were in imminent danger, and the horse was paralyzed with fright. When John tried to right things, he was caught under the wagon-host's gear. One of the black members of the party, named Burwell, saved the situation and their lives with great skill and bravery. The family was persuaded to remain on Clough Creek permanently by the Gwaltneys, who had come there from Isle of Wight County, Virginia, earlier and settled there. On September 12, 1803, John bought fifty-three acres from Josiah Gwaltney.

U.S. congressman John Claiborne graduated from the University of Pennsylvania's medical school in 1798 and became a physician. In 1804, he was elected to the U.S. House of Representatives as a Democratic-Republican. He was reelected in 1806 and served until his death on October 9, 1808. He was the son of Congressman Thomas Claiborne and is buried in the Jarrett Family Cemetery in Dinwiddie County.

During this period, the best means of transporting goods to market was by bateaux, lightweight boats with flat bottoms that could easily navigate the local rivers. The Upper Appomattox River Navigation Company, incorporated in 1795, made the river navigable by bateaux for 120 miles above Petersburg. A planned "Junction Canal," chartered in 1825 but never begun, would have connected the Appomattox River with the river trade of the Roanoke River. By 1820, more than three thousand bateau trips per year passed through Dinwiddie County.

Raceland, also known as Rice's Tavern, was built circa 1750. The building originally was a simple story-and-a-half dwelling, built by Peter Jones. It has since been transformed into a two-story Federal-style house. It has been used as a tavern and private home. William "Racer Billy" Wynn, owner of several fine horses in the early nineteenth century, once lived here. Wynn had stables, slaves and a racetrack on the property and briefly owned the famous racehorse Timoleon, considered one of the fastest Thoroughbreds of the 1810s. People from all over Virginia and North Carolina would come to the races held here and at the nearby tracks.

It was here that one of the most important early Virginia artifacts was unearthed: a copper badge issued by the Virginia General Assembly to the chief of the Appamattock Indians in 1662. It is now in the collection of the Jamestown-Yorktown Educational Trust after being purchased in a local auction just over a decade ago. In 1662, the Virginia General Assembly passed an act that required Indians visiting English settlements to display a copper or silver badge stating the name of the tribe to which they belonged. The badges were given to the chiefs of the Virginia Indian tribes that had signed treaties acknowledging the authority of Virginia's English government. The chiefs were responsible for issuing the badges to tribal members who had reason to travel in English-occupied parts of Virginia. It is one of only three of the twenty badges given to the Virginia Indian chiefs in 1662 known to survive today. The other two are both owned by the Virginia Historical Society. The whereabouts of a fourth badge last seen in 1888 are unknown. The Appamattock badge, like the other known Virginia badges of 1662, probably was made by an English/Scottish metalsmith working in Virginia.

The badge measures 2.25 inches by 1.65 inches and is pierced with two holes for suspension. The word "Appamattock" is inscribed on both faces of the badge, along with a decoration of plant tendrils. The badge was probably lost or discarded by the Appamattock Indians, who dwelled on the south side of the James River, near the present-day city of Petersburg, in the late seventeenth century. The act that mandated the use of the badges was repealed in 1694.

U.S. congressman Patrick Magruder attended Princeton College and later studied law and was admitted to the bar. He was elected to Congress from Maryland and served a single term from 1805 to 1807. He applied for the position of clerk of the House of Representatives in 1807 and that same year was appointed second librarian of Congress by President Thomas Jefferson. He filled both positions concurrently, from 1807 until his resignation due to poor health in 1815. Magruder then retired to Sweden, a plantation owned by his wife, in Dinwiddie County, where he died on December 24, 1819. He was buried in the Goodwyn family cemetery.

An all too often overlooked grave marker in Blandford Cemetery reads, "In Memory of General Joseph Jones of Cedar Grove, Petersburg, 1749–1824, Churchman, Patriot, Soldier, Vestryman of Bristol Parish 1773, Member of Committee of Public Safety 1775, Captain Virginia Line 1776–79, and Colonel of Militia 1793. Lieutenant and Member of House of Delegates, Dinwiddie Co., 1793, Major General 1802, Postmaster of Petersburg and Collector of Port 1821–24." This stone is part of the original Tomb at Cedar Grove, erected by Frances Bland Randolph Chapter DAR 1937. Jones also served as a justice of the Dinwiddie County Court in 1772, 1774, 1784 and 1789. He served as a member of the House of Delegates from Dinwiddie County from 1784 to 1787 and as the county's representative in the State Senate from Dinwiddie County from 1788 to 1790. He was sheriff of Dinwiddie County throughout 1789.

Matthew Lewis—a dark brown black man, five feet four and a half inches tall, fifty-three years old, born free and raised in Dinwiddie County—was a shoemaker. In 1804, he was just one of a few free blacks living in Dinwiddie County as an independent artisan.

Winfield Scott was a native of Dinwiddie County and first practiced law both in Dinwiddie County and Petersburg. James Hargrave, a local Quaker, was one of young Scott's earliest schoolteachers. At nineteen, he left the College of William and Mary and entered the law office of Judge David Robinson in Petersburg as a student. After practicing law, he entered the military and soon became a veteran of the War of 1812 and was considered

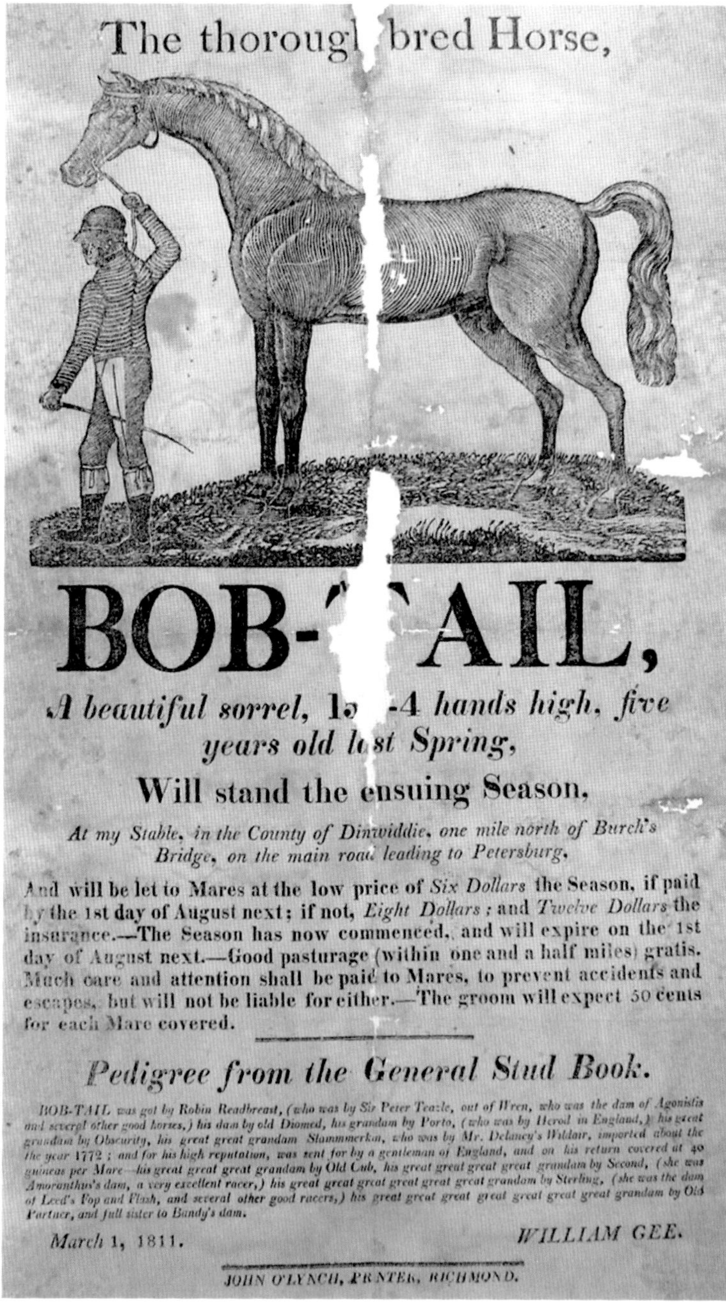
The thoroug[illegible] bred Horse,

BOB-TAIL,

A beautiful sorrel, 15 [illegible]-4 hands high, five years old last Spring,

Will stand the ensuing Season,

At my Stable, in the County of Dinwiddie, one mile north of Burch's Bridge, on the main road leading to Petersburg,

And will be let to Mares at the low price of *Six Dollars* the Season, if paid by the 1st day of August next; if not, *Eight Dollars*; and *Twelve Dollars* the insurance.—The Season has now commenced, and will expire on the 1st day of August next.—Good pasturage (within one and a half miles) gratis. Much care and attention shall be paid to Mares, to prevent accidents and escapes, but will not be liable for either.—The groom will expect 50 cents for each Mare covered.

Pedigree from the General Stud Book.

BOB-TAIL was got by Robin Readbreast, (who was by Sir Peter Teazle, out of Wren, who was the dam of Agonistis and several other good horses,) his dam by old Diomed, his grandam by Porto, (who was by Herod in England,) his great grandam by Obscurity, his great great grandam Slammerkin, who was by Mr. Delancy's Wildair, imported about the the year 1772; and for his high reputation, was sent for by a gentleman of England, and on his return covered at 40 guineas per Mare—his great great great grandam by Old Cub, his great great great great grandam by Second, (she was Amoranthus's dam, a very excellent racer,) his great great great great great great grandam by Sterling, (she was the dam of Leed's Fop and Flash, and several other good racers,) his great great great great great great great grandam by Old Partner, and full sister to Bandy's dam.

March 1, 1811. *WILLIAM GEE.*

JOHN O'LYNCH, PRINTER, RICHMOND.

March 1, 1811 broadside entitled "BOB-TAIL…At my stable, in the County of Dinwiddie, one mile north of Burch's Bridge, on the main road leading to Petersburg…William Gee." *Author's collection.*

Winfield Scott. *Courtesy of the Library of Congress.*

a hero during the Mexican War. General Winfield Scott was later the Union's senior commander at the very start of the Civil War, having served fourteen presidents, beginning with Thomas Jefferson. His failure to join the Confederate army caused many Dinwiddians to informally banish him from his native county. Then at age seventy-five, Scott was known as "Old Fuss and Feathers" for his strict attention to military codes of dress and conduct. He was in declining health; gout and dropsy, coupled with the corpulence of his six-foot, five-inch frame, had reduced him to being an armchair general. Still, Scott's mind was alert and focused on military matters. Although his "Anaconda Plan," which would blockade the enemy's seaports and divide the Confederacy in two by taking control of the Mississippi River, appeared to be largely impractical at the start, it ultimately proved to be a winning strategy for the Union.

Dinwiddie County and Petersburg were unique because of their pro-black environments supporting large free black populations, and both were generally supportive of the colonization movement. Surrounding counties of Chesterfield, Prince George, Amelia, Nottoway, Brunswick and Greensville

General Joseph Jones's remains were moved from Cedar Grove to Blandford Cemetery in Petersburg, Virginia. *Author's collection.*

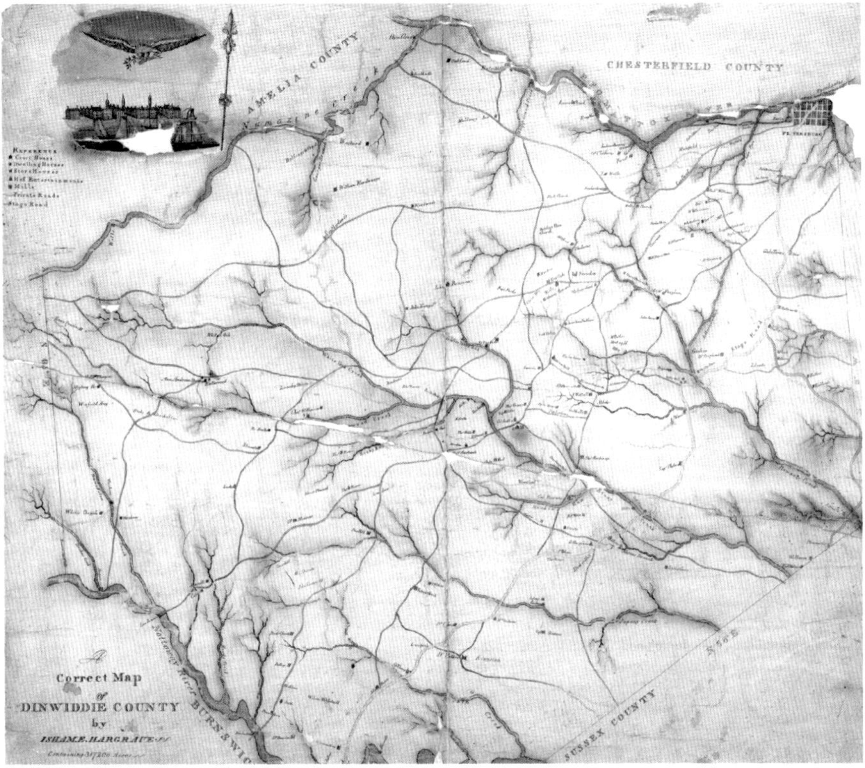

1820 map.

didn't develop Colonization Auxiliary Societies; only neighboring Sussex County, Petersburg (1823) and Dinwiddie County (1826) established Auxiliary Colonization Societies.

In 1818, Rebecca Hanson was registered as a free woman of color, "five feet two inches high, forty years old, brown complexion, rather light." She had been born free in Dinwiddie County. Free blacks had to register with local courts and always be able to prove their status if questioned. Being a free black didn't mean one was truly free or equal. Lives still remained harsh and quite restrictive.

St. George Tucker served as the Dinwiddie County Court clerk in 1774, having finished his law studies with the eminent lawyer George Wythe in Williamsburg. When Lord Dunmore dissolved the House of Burgesses, Tucker's law license and clerkship became worthless. In 1778, Tucker's courtship of Frances Bland Randolph resulted in their marriage. They lived at Matoax, a 1,300-acre Chesterfield County estate nestled along the Appomattox River's northern bank near Petersburg.

He would later move his family to Williamsburg to teach law at William and Mary.

The American Colonization Society of Petersburg was formed in 1823, with Dr. Richard Field, president; vice-presidents John F. May and Reverend Andrew Syme; Gabriel P. Disosway, treasurer; and Thomas Shore, secretary. The group helped the seventeen free blacks expatriated from Petersburg's area to gain passage on the brig *Oswego*, which left Baltimore on April 13, 1823, and arrived at Monrovia, Africa, on May 24, 1823. Details on their travel to Baltimore are uncertain, but they probably sailed to Baltimore on one of the many schooners leaving Petersburg.

Later, the ship *Cyrus* was berthed along the wharf at City Point, Prince George County, having just returned from a long voyage in November. About 106 free blacks left onboard the *Cyrus*, about January 1, 1824, from City Point, arriving at Monrovia, Africa, on February 13, 1824. Most had been residents of Petersburg and Dinwiddie County. City Point was little more than a very small village, with about two dozen structures and several deep-water berthing wharfs controlled by various Petersburg-based merchants; large vessels couldn't make the longer journey up the adjacent Appomattox River, so those with cargos going to Petersburg would be reloaded here on smaller vessels. It wouldn't be until 1838 when the train from Petersburg would finally reach City Point and foster its overall growth.

The Dinwiddie Auxiliary Colonization Society was organized on July 1, 1826, at the Butterwood Meeting House at the first-anniversary meeting of the Butterwood Auxiliary Bible Society in western Dinwiddie County. A constitution was adopted, and the following officers were elected for the ensuring year: Daniel Gilman Hatch, president; William B. Thompson, vice-president; Isa A. Easter, treasurer; Robert H. Booth, secretary; and managers Robert C. Booth, Joseph H. Harper, Stith Thompson, John Wainwright, John Atkinson, Douglass Muir, Wm. H. Cousins, John N. Fisher, Robert V. Tucker, Dodson Worsham and Henry C. Worsham.

Stith Thompson, Daniel G. Hatch and Robert H. Booth were appointed to a committee to attend the secession of the parent colonization society and report the state of this society. Benjamin Garlner, Esq., was appointed to deliver a suitable discourse at the next anniversary meeting of the society, which was scheduled to take place at Winfield Academy on the following Fourth of July.

In 1828, the Dinwiddie Auxiliary Colonization Society was composed of Daniel Gilman Hatch, president; William B. Thompson, vice-president; Robert H. Booth, secretary; and Beverly Anderson, treasurer. The society had elected the following managers: John Wainwright, John Atkinson,

Robert C. Booth, Douglass Muir, W.H. Cousins, John N. Fisher, Robert V. Tucker, Stith Thompson and Joseph H. Harper. Records of this society are scant, but its mere existence is remarkable and reflective of the discourse over slavery here within the county.

The *Republican Compiler* of Gettysburg, Pennsylvania, would report on January 18, 1826, that a massive fire occurred in Petersburg on January 5:

> *Great Calamity! It is our painful duty to describe for the information of distant readers, one of the greatest calamities which have befallen our borough since the desolating scene of 1815. On Wednesday night, about 7 o'clock our citizens were aroused by the alarm of fire. The flames were soon discovered to burst with a great volume from the sides and roof of the lumber house owned by Messrs. Mabry & Dugger, in rear of their store on Old street; and in a few minutes, notwithstanding the greatest exertions were used, caught a number of similar buildings adjacent. At this moment, the wind, previously from the north, changed to the North east and appeared to increase in violence as the flames progressed.*
>
> *In a little time no less than six houses were on fire and presented an awful spectacle indeed—a stream of ascended flame illuminated the heavens to the utmost verge of the horizon; and large fire-brands, with innumerable cinders and sparks were observed coursing the air for hundreds and thousands of yards. Never before was such a sight presented to our eyes. It seemed to be a combination of elements to work our destruction; a storm of wind accompanied by a shower of fire!*
>
> *In all about forty buildings were consumed. Those of the better kind for the most part were insured. The principal individual loss consists in groceries, produce &c. stored in the lumber houses. It is impracticable as yet to estimate accurately the amount.*
>
> *For circumstances there is no doubt entertained that this scene of wide-spread destruction was the work of some vile incendiary, as reckless as wicked. The author as yet has eluded discovery but we trust in the justice of Providence to drag him into open day that he may meet the punishment due to one of the blackest of crimes.*

Then again on July 21, 1826, there were reports of yet another fire:

> *Our unfortunate Borough would seem to be devoted to destruction! In our last Tuesday's paper, we gave our readers an account of a conflagration which commenced in rear of Sycamore street just as a large portion of our Citizens*

> *were about to engage in the funeral services and ceremonies appointed to be performed at Blandford Church in respect and honor of the memory of the departed worthies, Jefferson and Adams by which about twenty buildings were destroyed: and now we have to perform the unpleasant task of announcing another similar occurrence by which a still greater loss of property has been sustained. On Tuesday morning, about half past 11 o'clock, a fire broke out in a range of wooden buildings opposite West-Hill Warehouse on Walnut Street, generally known by the name of Allison's Row. These Houses were erected after the great fire of 1815, were put up in haste for the accommodations of the sufferers by that calamity and having been built of combustible materials, at the time in a very dry state, the flames spread both North and South with extraordinary velocity. In less than an hour, notwithstanding every effort was made to suppress the fire, the whole range was reduced to ashes. The number of houses destroyed, large and small, was about 30, nearly all built of wood. They were for the most part insured; but being generally occupied by indigent families, there are doubtless instances of severe individual suffering caused by this visitation. As to the origin of the fire, nothing is certainly known, except that it commenced in a bake house.*

On July 30, 1826, fire struck again:

> *Well may it be said that Petersburg appears to be a devoted town for another FIRE broke out there on Monday morning the 30th ultimo, between 1 and 2 o'clock which consumed, it is understood, from twenty-five to thirty buildings. Fortunately however, they were all of wood and not probably of more than two thousand dollars value, the whole of them. Mr. J. V. Wilcox lost his warehouse, which was the greatest individual loss, but its contents had been previously removed. 500 bales of cotton were in imminent danger but were saved. The fire originated in a* [Black] *hut in Beard's alley between Bank and Old streets and was not doubt the work of an incendiary and the houses destroyed were pretty much of the character of the one first fired or worse and it is said their tenants were mostly the offal's of society.*
>
> *A respectable resident of Petersburg states that many of the blacks of that town are forted and make a part of the fire companies and that it is customary to give those members a holiday, the day succeeding a fire, besides paying them for their services to help to extinguish it and save property.*

Rebuilding occurred, with many homes and businesses being insured against fire by the Mutual Assurance Society of Virginia in Richmond and being generally rebuilt in brick, not wood. During this period, residents started to move from farming toward developing industrial goods and services. Thus there was a need to upgrade general educational goals. The Quakers had already provided sectarian education for boys at a school on Quaker Road, several miles northeast of the courthouse, starting about 1800. Other institutions for boys were the Dinwiddie Academy, located at the courthouse and opened in 1812 with Jonathan Smith as principal; the Winfield Academy, founded in 1819 at Darvills Plantation; and Dr. Paterson Harper's Academy, begun in the western part of the county in about 1820. Dinwiddie Academy offered studies in Latin, Greek, geography, belles-lettres, history, logic, mathematics and natural and moral philosophy. Winfield Academy was held in a two-story building with a ground floor made of stone and containing a single room heated by fireplaces at both ends and a two-room frame second floor. It would remain open until 1848.

Not until the end of the eighteenth century did Virginia even begin to consider the creation of a public school system. The state act of 1796 promoting education, including a provision to provide schooling for the poor, was left to the justices of the counties to implement. There is little evidence that Dinwiddie embraced the concept of public education. During the next fifty years, the Virginia Assembly continued to strengthen the newly emerging public schools. The Literary Fund was created in 1810 and set up to distribute money to counties to educate only poor white children. In 1819, the state's Literary Fund was made available to increase teachers' pay in public schools. There was prejudice against the free school idea in the antebellum period, and there is little evidence that such schools were popular anywhere in the state, let alone in Dinwiddie County. No school building of this period survives in the county today.

By 1830, Dinwiddie County's population had reached a stable level of around 5,257, and Petersburg's census was counted on its own. Petersburg then dominated the county's commercial trade. Other than the central courthouse village on the southern Stage Road, there were few settlements, mostly nodes on major transportation routes. A few villages grew up at transportation or industrial hubs. These included Goodwynsville and Harrisville or Wyoming on the Nottoway River where the Stage Road crossed the river, Poplar Grove, Richieville and Sappony Creeks. Wyoming contained a small mercantile store, a blacksmith shop, a wheelwright shop and two nearby manufacturing mills, while the others contained only a post office and probably a small, poorly stocked country store.

Historians have generally overlooked John Day, a free Dinwiddie black whose mother was of Indian ancestry. He was a cabinetmaker, along with his brother Thomas, who was a renowned North Carolina furniture maker who sent his children to private school in the North. Both men were raised in Dinwiddie County. John later became a Baptist minister and immigrated to Liberia in 1830 with his wife and four children. His wife and kids died within a short time of their arrival, and he would go on to become superintendent of the Baptist Mission there and later chief justice of the Liberia Supreme Court. In 1804, his grandfather, Dr. Thomas Stewart, a free black in Dinwiddie County, recorded Stewart's African ancestral name, Thody, in his will—a truly rare occurrence. The Stewart-Day family warrants further scholarly study than is available within this book.

Throughout the rural parts of the United States, legal tender was scarce until nearly the end of the nineteenth century. It seems that barter formed one of the principal means of exchange in these areas. The merchant was a central figure in the local economy, exchanging goods for the farmer's surplus produce and extending credit. Similarly, gristmills provided a service in exchange for a toll or a portion of the product. This commercial system insulated the local economy from the fluctuations of the national cash system. The relative nearness of Petersburg, however, meant that the city's economy would reach out into Dinwiddie County and beyond.

Care of the poor and helpless of the immediate area was the responsibility of the local Anglican parish vestry under colonial law. After the Revolution, that responsibility passed to county officials called the overseers of the poor.

Various artisans and mechanics began making a living in the county during this period. They included John Andrews, a cabinetmaker, textile machinery maker, inventor and turner; Joseph Jones, a silversmith or jeweler; William Reamy, a cabinetmaker; Sterling H. Woodward, a coach or riding chair maker and Windsor chair maker; and Henry Evans and Benjamin Conway, who were wheelwrights. Also of note were various enslaved mechanics such as Fed, a blacksmith who ran away in 1801, and Ned, a blacksmith who ran away in 1804. Their only recordings would be their rewards posted in area papers.

As early as September 1829, business interests in Petersburg wanted to build a railroad between Petersburg, Virginia, and Weldon, North Carolina. The railroad would connect the Appomattox and Roanoke Rivers and attract trade away from Norfolk, Virginia, which was connected to North Carolina by a canal. The Petersburg and Weldon Railroad was incorporated on February 10, 1830, making it one of the earliest railroads in the United States. By 1833, a trip could be made along sixty miles of the line.

Chapter 4

ANTEBELLUM PERIOD

1831–1860

Various hamlets across the county served as the sites of post offices, stores, taverns and mills. In 1835, post offices were located at the Dinwiddie hamlet, Goodwynsville, Wyoming, Poplar Grove, Richieville and Sappony Creek. Only Wyoming had reached the size of a village by 1835. Among the most important of these tiny communities in 1835 was the centrally placed Dinwiddie Courthouse, which had a tavern to serve the citizens for court-day appearances, and Wyoming, with a mercantile store, a blacksmith shop, a wheelwright and two nearby manufacturing mills.

James Stanton (1779–1852) was a Dinwiddie Quaker and minister to African Americans and Native Americans. He was born to Quaker parents, James and Ann Stanton. He was brother to John, born October 7, 1777; William, born November 16, 1782; Frederick, born February 2, 1784; Mary, born March 28, 1786; and Robert, born July 17, 1788, and all of these births were recorded in the Blackwater Monthly Meeting records of Southside Virginia.

James Stanton achieved considerable success in assisting Virginia's black population. He was well known as an abolitionist and member of the Society of Friends (Orthodox). In 1826, James Stanton, at age forty-three, and his family moved to Warren County, Ohio, and purchased a 114-acre farm in Clear Creek Township. The farm, known as Greenhill Farm, was a station on the Underground Railroad. The house is listed on the National Registry of Historic Places. In 1828, Stanton was a member of the Society of Friends of Indiana Yearly Meeting, and he attended the

Mount Pleasant meetinghouse, where he served on a committee on Indian concerns. Stanton was a lay preacher in the Society of Friends and made many trips among the Indians of the Miami Valley and as far away as the Oklahoma Territory. He married Ann Jones, and they had a daughter, Catherine Ann, who was six years old when she and her family came to Ohio from Virginia in 1826. He and his niece Ann Stanton assisted Elizabeth Harvey and her family after her husband, Dr. Jesse Harvey, of Harveysburg, Ohio, died in 1849.

Dinwiddie County, except for the village of Blandford, was the parent of the town of Petersburg until 1850, when the legislature granted a charter making Petersburg an independent city. Dinwiddians, in tracing the history of their county up to 1850, should bear in mind that the events and the people living in Petersburg up to that time were an inseparable part of greater Dinwiddie County.

By 1850, the villages and crossroads hamlets had grown a little. Thomson's Mercantile and Professional Directory of 1851 indicates that there were four stores in the courthouse community: S.S. Baker; Peebles and Sturdivant; John Perkins; and James M. Williams. John W. Butterworth and Archibald Thweat operated stores at Wyoming, and John Hogwood had a store at Fork Inn (Sutherland). The courthouse was home to two attorneys at law: Isaac S. Keeler and E.B. Worsham. Physicians were found near Mount Pleasant, Fork Inn, Richieville, Darvills and Wyoming. The county's only hotel was located at the courthouse and operated by William H. Goodyer.

The closeness of Petersburg made it unnecessary to organize a bank in the county, unlike in western Virginia, where branches of eastern banks were opened during the antebellum period. With no bank in the county, local farmers and storekeepers with capital acted as bankers, holding mortgages and making loans. Regional commerce became increasingly important as transportation improved. Petersburg's powerful economy continued to dominate the region. Similarly, the county government experienced a limited expansion in the antebellum period.

The frame courthouse built in the 1820s stood until 1849. In 1851, a new Greek Revival–style Dinwiddie County Courthouse was erected on the same spot. The building did not include the columned portico, which was added in the twentieth century. The county seat continued to be a regional political center, with monthly court days. The courthouse square was surrounded by a few businesses and houses. In 1858, a second floor was inserted in the high-ceilinged original courtroom, providing offices and jury rooms on the first floor and a courtroom on the second.

The need for better transportation routes was a primary concern during this period. An act passed by the Virginia General Assembly in 1835 gave responsibility for road maintenance to the counties through a direct tax or levy and permitted the hiring of road workers. Regional turnpikes began to link localities in central Virginia with a transportation network connecting the region with eastern markets.

Road improvements, as they occurred, also meant better river crossings. Improved roads further reinforced the status of the county seat as the nexus of commerce for the locality and continued to serve exclusively as local transportation routes supplementing river and rail travel until the coming of the railroad in the late nineteenth century.

Education during this period followed earlier trends, but a gradual improvement followed the establishment of voluntary state guidelines and the availability of building funds after 1829, though this generally applied only to white children. In compliance with state directives designed to encourage citizens to voluntarily improve educational opportunities, counties were supposed to divide themselves into school districts. All white children over the age of six were to receive education free of charge. This took the form of a per diem paid to aid poor students. Dinwiddie County officials took advantage of public funding to supplement educational opportunities. By 1850, there were about a dozen common schools and several girls' schools receiving some public funding. Several academies operating outside Petersburg also received some public funds.

The county still had several private academies: Jefferson Academy on Cox's Road; Green Wood Seminary, at the courthouse; and Olden Place Seminary, near Drills, all in a flourishing condition, and there were also many normal schools. Others founded in the antebellum period include the Mt. Liberty School, Wyoming School, Fleetwood Academy and Charles Young's Academy. As time passed, education for young women was seen as desirable by wealthy families. A girl's education could be provided at schools such as the Female Academy, opened in 1839, and the Olden Place Female Seminary, started in 1840 near Darvills, mentioned previously. Other girls' institutions included Girard Heartwell's School for Girls and Oak Forest Female School. No school building from this period still stands, and the lack of education for black children should be apparent. At best, it was left to the parents to home-school their own children.

Agriculture continued as the primary occupation in antebellum Dinwiddie County. There were 750 active farms in 1850. The lands of this county were generally poor but rich in clay, except along the Nottoway River and in the vicinity of Petersburg, where they were much improved in antebellum Dinwiddie. The prime products were tobacco, cotton and wheat. The farms and historic roads through the county form the principal elements in the historic agricultural landscape that defines the county to this day. In 1850, twenty-four churches were recorded, including seventeen Methodist, three Baptist, two Episcopal, one Quaker and one Campbellite Baptist (Disciples of Christ).

The family farm continued to characterize the lives of most residents, although slavery and the plantation system held sway in some areas, particularly along the Appomattox River. As was true throughout the region, most slave owners held one or two slaves and worked beside them in the house or field. At the same time, a few major owners had large numbers of enslaved workers. Dinwiddie continued to see advancement in the number of free blacks who owned land.

Industry became much more diversified in the antebellum era, with a number of highly capitalized companies beginning operation. Mills ranged from the local gristmill to large commercial mills. The 1850 U.S. Industrial Census provides information about the state of industry in the Dinwiddie of the 1850s. In addition to the twenty-one mills listed, there were three tanners and shoemakers, fourteen blacksmiths, six barrel and box makers, one coach factory, two quarries and four wheelwrights. There were five sawmills, one lumbering business and one carpenter. Sadly, nearly all traces of these activities during this period have since vanished from the landscape.

An example of this upward movement of the time was Robert Clark, who began with little capital and even less experience. After working in a hotel and saving enough to purchase his freedom, he opened a livery stable, which eventually became the most popular establishment of its kind in the town of Petersburg. By 1860, he possessed a total estate of $9,000, including $5,000 worth of real estate.

Chapter 5

CIVIL WAR

1861–1865

The Civil War adversely affected Dinwiddie County in particularly violent ways, though one positive outcome was the forced freeing of its enslaved population. As in most parts of Virginia, the products of the countryside were depleted in service of the Confederate cause. Many local soldiers died. However, the important railroad lines through the county and the nearness of the final target of Grant's army at Petersburg caused a long series of battles to be fought across the county in the final month of the war. Almost every public and large private building was said to have been used as a hospital by one side or the other after the several major battles.

Historians generally agree that economic conflicts were not a major cause of the war. Economic historian Lee A. Craig reports, "In fact, numerous studies by economic historians over the past several decades reveal that economic conflict was not an inherent condition of North–South relations during the antebellum era and did not cause the Civil War. When numerous groups tried at the last minute in 1860–61 to find a compromise to avert war, they did not turn to economic policies. Aside from the economic institution of slavery, no other economic issues brought about the Civil War."

However, to estimate the war's cost is an extremely difficult task. Very questionable assumptions, interpolations and several extrapolations arise as to the true cost to our society, but one is forced also to price the priceless, setting a monetary value on hundreds of thousands of lives lost and displaced. Not surprisingly, many scholars still skirt the issue of the American Civil War's costs. Instead, they state with some magnitude that the war cost a lot but act as

General Robert E. Lee. *Courtesy of U.S. Army History and Education Center.*

though the only responsibility worthy of serious scholarship is General Lee's troop movements. Those left behind paid a price as well; enduring great hardship and witnessing a tragic conflict unfolding before their eyes are all too often overlooked.

The *Richmond Enquirer* reported on Saturday morning, March 23, 1861:

> *The True Issue—The issue to be decided by the people of Virginia is clearly stated in the following resolution, adopted by public meeting in the county of Dinwiddie: "Resolved, 1st. The old Union being irreparably dissolved, there is no option left us, save to unite our destinies with our sister Southern States—or, to remain a useless appendage to the Northern Confederacy—the latter alternative being utterly repugnant to ALL TRUE SOUTHERN MEN." Here is a noble platform for the Resistance Party of Virginia. The question of secession is not before the people of Virginia—it has been decided, and they have now to choose between the Confederate States of the South and the Northern Union. The old Union, the glorious Union our fathers made, has been dissolved—ruthlessly torn asunder by Northern fanaticism—against the earnest protestation of the people of Virginia. From that Union, the allies of Virginia, her truth and mien have been derived, and her people have now to decide whether they will remain with the North or go with the South. The agitation of secession is the agitation of a question decided, and which can be remedied by no determination of Virginia. She did not dissolve the Union, and she cannot restore it. The North has disrupted the Union, and only the Northern States can re-construct it. The Northern States have driven the Southern States out; the Northern States must bring back the Southern States. Virginia's ultimatum with a Border State Conference is a loss of time, a waste of paper, useless for all purposes, save those of Mr. Seward, "delay" and "wait."—We are not without an ultimatum which will re-construct the Union; the States sought to be brought back are the only parties whose ultimatum can restore the Union. Virginia's ultimatum may determine the conditions upon which she will remain with the North, but further than this it cannot go; if the re-construction of the old Union is the real object of the Convention, the adoption of the ultimatum of the seceded States will attest its sincerity and convince the people of the country that they are not scheming for party purpose, and that they have not given up to party the time and labor they were directed to bestow upon the country. The ultimatum of the seceded States is left in no uncertainty; it is to be found in the solemn action of the Montgomery Constitution and may be analyzed as follows:*

That African slavery in the Territories shall be recognized and protected by Congress and the Territorial Legislatures.

That the right to slaveholders of transit and sojourn in any State of the Confederacy, with their slaves and other property, shall be recognized and respected.

That the provision in regard to fugitive slaves shall extend to any slave lawfully carried from one State into another, and there escaping or taken away from his master.

That no bill or ex post facto law (by Congress or any State,) and no law impairing or denying the right of property in Negro slaves, shall be passed.

That the African slave trade shall be prohibited by such laws of Congress as shall effectually prevent the same.

The report made by Virginia Gov. Henry Wise embraces all these. The Convention, in voting upon the report of Gov. Wise, will decide for or against the Northern Confederacy. Gov. Wise presents no question of secession, he accepts that as already decided, and calls upon the Convention of Virginia to declare either for the old Union upon the ultimatum laid down by the seceded States; or for Union with the seceded, or for remaining with the North. In voting down the report of Gov. Wise and adopting that of the majority, the Convention will have deliberately voted down the only plan of re-construction; they will also have voted down the Union with the South; and they will have decided, without consulting the people of Virginia, to remain "a useless appendage to the Northern Confederacy," an "alternative utterly repugnant to all true Southern men." Our connection with the Federal Union has been dissolved by the disruption of the Union, but Virginia is under the dominion and government of the Northern States, according to the forms of the Constitution of the once Federal Union. Shall she so remain? The Convention, by adopting the majority report, will determine this question in favor of the North. Will the people ratify such action by the Convention? The question does not involve secession or disunion, but merely whether, the Union being dissolved, Virginia will remain with the North or go with the South. Such is the issue between the resistance and submission parties in Virginia.

In the end, Dinwiddie County was the scene of forty-nine battles, engagements and skirmishes, with over fifty miles of fortifications and sixty forts and batteries, overall perhaps the largest battlefield in America. Many of its men served, including General Roger Atkinson Pryor, who was born on July 19, 1828. Pryor was educated in 1845 at Hampden-Sydney College and in 1848 at the University of Virginia, graduating with a degree in law. He was admitted to the Virginia bar in 1849. Though he had studied law, he became a journalist as a staff member of the *Washington Union* and in 1853 became editor of the *Richmond Enquirer*. In 1855, at age twenty-seven, he was sent to Greece by President Pierce as a special commissioner. On his return, he established a political journal at Richmond, called *The South*, in which he represented the views of Virginia.

Roger Atkinson Pryor was a supporter of states' rights for the South. In 1859, General Pryor was elected to the U.S. House of Representatives and reelected in 1860 to a second term, but due to the secession of Virginia from the Union, he resigned. He then served in the Provisional Confederate Congress (1861) and the First Regular Congress (1862). He played a prominent part in the proceedings of the Charleston Democratic Convention in 1860 and became an advocate for the Southern Confederacy. Pryor went to Charleston as a member of the staff of General Beauregard. He witnessed the bombardment of Fort Sumter on April 12. At Fort Johnson, the order to open fire on Fort Sumter was given to Captain George S. James, a great admirer of Pryor, who offered Pryor the privilege, but Pryor responded, "I could not fire the first gun of war." Pryor entered the Confederate army as a colonel and soon became a brigadier general. He commanded the Third Virginia Regiment at Portsmouth, taking part in the Battles of Yorktown, Williamsburg, Seven Pines, Second Bull Run and Antietam. After Antietam, his regiment was disassembled, and he then resigned his commission and served at the request of General Robert E. Lee doing both scouting and intelligence work. He was captured in November 1864 and made a prisoner at Fort Lafayette in New York.

After the war, Pryor and his wife, Sara—both members of the Southern aristocracy and with strong relationships with Stephen A. Douglas and Robert E. Lee—set about restoring their lives. They moved to New York City, where Pryor entered the practice of law, being appointed to the New York Court of Common Pleas (1890), the New York State Supreme Court (1896) and the Appellate Division of the New York Supreme Court (1899–1919). He died on March 14, 1919. There have been several books published about their lives and accomplishments, the most recent being *Surviving the Confederacy: Rebellion, Ruin and Recovery—Roger and Sara Pryor During the Civil War*, by John C. Waugh.

In June 1864, to deny General Robert E. Lee the use of the South Side Railroad and the Richmond and Danville Railroad, General Ulysses S. Grant sent General James H. Wilson and General August V. Kautz south of

Petersburg on a cavalry raid to destroy track and rolling stock. The Eleventh Pennsylvania Cavalry, the advance guard of the Wilson-Kautz column, arrived here at Reams Station about 7:30 a.m. on June 22 and burned the station and other buildings along the Petersburg and Weldon Railroad. General James Dearing's eight-hundred-man cavalry brigade of General W.H.F. "Rooney" Lee's cavalry division was alerted, and it engaged the rear of Wilson's column in a running skirmish that continued some ten miles to Dinwiddie courthouse. Reams Station was guarded by a small body of local militia. A portion of them were captured, and the remainder dispersed. Here the sad but necessary work of destruction began. All the buildings at the station, together with a locomotive and a train of five or six cars, were consigned to the flames.

Edward P. Tobie, First Maine Cavalry, wrote home:

> *The enemy's pickets were encountered near the Jerusalem Plank Road* [U.S. Route 301], *and were pursued to Reams Station, several were captured along the way. General Kautz's orders were to move to Southerland's along the South Side Railroad, but the captured pickets informed him that General W.H.F. Lee, with two brigades of cavalry, was encamped in the path he was ordered to take. Being unwilling to jeopardize the mission at the beginning by encouraging an engagement, General Kautz turned the head of his column down the Weldon road, as if that was the object of the raid.*

The Battle of Globe Tavern, also known as the Second Battle of the Weldon Railroad, over August 18–21, 1864, south of Petersburg, was the second attempt of the Union army to split the Weldon Railroad during the Siege of Petersburg. A Union force under Major General Gouverneur K. Warren destroyed miles of track and withstood attacks from Confederate troops under General P.G.T. Beauregard and Lieutenant General A.P. Hill. It was the first Union victory in the Richmond-Petersburg Campaign. It forced the Confederates to carry their supplies thirty miles by wagon to bypass the new Union lines that were extended farther to the south and west.

The Second Battle of Reams Station was fought on August 25, 1864. Major General Winfield S. Hancock's Union forces began destroying the Weldon Railroad tracks, which served as a vital supply line for General Robert E. Lee's Confederate army in Petersburg. Lee sent Lieutenant General A.P. Hill forces to challenge Hancock; the Confederates were able to rout the Union troops from their earthen fortifications at Reams Station. Next, Hill

Globe Tavern. *Courtesy of the Library of Congress.*

was to take advantage of the units Lee had removed from his right to retake Fort Harrison. Warren's attack was aimed at the fortifications guarding the Boydton Plank Road, which was being used to carry supplies into Petersburg from the Confederate railhead at Stony Creek to the south. This line was being extended to reach the vicinity of the Union flank at Globe Tavern. A temporary line was held along the Squirrel Level Road.

On September 30, Robert E. Lee attempted to retake Fort Harrison, and Warren and Gregg began marching along the Poplar Springs Road toward the Squirrel Level Road line in the area of Peebles' Farm and Poplar Springs Church. Lee had pulled forces from this flank for the counterattack on Fort Harrison, so Warren was marching against Lieutenant General A.P. Hill's reduced corps. Around 1:00 p.m., Brigadier General Charles Griffin led the assault against the Confederates near the Poplar Springs Church. Griffin quickly captured Fort Archer on the extreme Confederate flank, and the Squirrel Level Road line broke and fled so quickly that few prisoners were captured. Warren halted the attack to fortify the new position in front of the Ninth Corps. The Union attack forced Lee to recall the Light Division from its march toward Fort Harrison. The Ninth Corps under Major General John G. Parke moved up on Warren's left but did not make an effective link with the Fifth Corps flank. Major General Henry Heth was preparing to mount a counterattack, which came and routed the Ninth Corps and forced one of its brigades to surrender. Warren, who had originally feared a counterattack, now helped rally the broken Ninth Corps units and check Heth's attack, and the fighting died down. Heth tried another flank attack the following day, which was repulsed, as was a cavalry attack under Major

The Battle of Peebles' Farm. *Courtesy of the Library of Congress.*

General Wade Hampton. On October 2, the Union position was reinforced by Brigadier General Gershom Mott's division from the Second Corps. Mott spearheaded a Union attack that day, which was aimed for the Boydton Plank Road. The attack easily overran Fort McRae but was checked before it reached the Boydton Plank Road. The Confederate defenders lost works on both sides of their lines. The Union army extended the siege lines past the Peebles' Farm area, bringing them all closer to their goal of cutting the Boydton Plank Road. The Union army was firmly entrenched in the area, and later that month the Second Corps would make an attempt to cut the Boydton Plank Road.

The Battle of the Boydton Plank Road (aka Burgess Mill or First Hatcher's Run), fought on October 27–28, 1864, was an attempt by the Union army to seize the Boydton Plank Road and cut the South Side Railroad, a critical supply line to Petersburg, Virginia. On October 27, Hancock marched across Hatcher's Run, brushed aside Confederate pickets and moved around the Confederate flank toward Burgess Mill. The division under Brigadier General Gershom Mott crossed the Boydton Plank Road and attacked Major General Wade Hampton's Confederate cavalry, attempting to cut it off from the main Confederate lines. Lieutenant General A.P. Hill, who commanded the Confederate defenses in the area, reacted quickly to Hancock's threat. However, once his units moved to confront the Union forces, Hill, in ill health, turned over the direction of his corps to Major General Henry Heth. Heth put two divisions in Hancock's path, but the Union commander drove up the Boydton Plank Road and pushed aside the opposing Confederates. At this time, both Major General George G. Meade and Lieutenant General Ulysses S. Grant rode out to the battlefield, where Meade immediately noticed a gap between Hancock and the Fifth Corps. With the South Side Railroad still six miles away, Meade realized that continuing the advance would only further isolate the Second Corps and so ordered Hancock to halt. Brigadier General Samuel W. Crawford's Fifth Corps division was ordered to connect with the Second Corps but became caught up in the dense woods. General Grant, meanwhile, made a personal reconnaissance of the Confederate works and determined that the Confederates were too strong and called off the offensive.

Having never connected with Crawford's division, Hancock's corps returned to Hatcher's Run crossing but found it blocked by Confederate cavalry. This left the Second Corps isolated on the north side of Hatcher's Run. Heth and Hampton saw a golden opportunity to destroy the whole Second Corps. Hancock's only line of retreat was the Dabney Mill Road, for which Heth was now aiming. Late in the afternoon, Brigadier General William Mahone's division attacked through the same woods that had stopped Crawford and seized the Dabney Mill Road, while a Confederate cavalry division under Major General W.H.F. "Rooney" Lee moved up behind the Union forces. Mahone moved so far around the Union flank that Brigadier General Thomas W. Egan's Second Corps division was forced to completely change fronts. Hancock was now surrounded on three sides with no line of retreat. But unlike at Reams Station, the Second Corps did not panic, and Hancock seized the initiative. Mahone was also nearly successful and found his division isolated in turn. Hancock ordered an attack on both Confederate flanks. Hampton failed to hold off the Union cavalry, and Gregg was able to move up and help to rout Mahone. The tables turned, and the Confederates, now threatened with encirclement, retreated up the Boydton Plank Road. Hancock retained his hold on the Boydton Plank Road, and Grant left to him the decision whether to remain or withdraw to the initial Union lines. Although Hancock had repulsed the Confederate attack, his position was still very unstable. That night, Hancock marched his men back to their original position.

The historical marker for the Battle of Hatcher's Run is on property owned by the Civil War Preservation Trust. *Photo by author.*

The Battle of Hatcher's Run, also known as Dabney's Mill, Armstrong's Mill, Rowanty Creek and Vaughn Road, was fought over February 5–7, 1865. Its aim was to cut off the Confederate supply line on Boydton Plank Road and the Weldon Railroad west of Petersburg, Virginia. On February 5, Gregg's cavalry division rode west to Dinwiddie Courthouse and the Boydton Plank Road via the Malone Road, two miles south of Reams Station. The Fifth Corps, under the command of Major General Gouverneur K. Warren, rode southwest toward Dinwiddie Courthouse via Rowanty Post Office/Billup's Post Office (Old Stage Road), one mile north of Reams Station. The Fifth Corps crossed Rowanty Creek at Monk's Neck Bridge and took up an obstructing position on the Vaughan Road between Gravelly and Little Cattail Runs to protect Gregg's right flank and prevent delay with the operations. Two divisions of the Second Corps under Major General Andrew A. Humphreys moved from the Halifax Road down the Vaughan Road to Hatcher's Run and shifted west to Armstrong's Mill, north of the Run, to cover Warren's right flank. Late in the day, Confederate major general John B. Gordon attacked the Second Corps from the north and attempted to turn Humphreys's right flank near the mill but was rejected. During the night, the Second Corps was reinforced by both Gregg's and the Fifth Corps cavalry, which had returned to the Vaughan Road after finding little supply-wagon traffic on the Boydton Plank Road. This now extended the Union line just south of Hatcher's Run.

On February 6, the Fifth Corps lines were attacked by units of Confederate brigadier general John Pegram's division. The Confederates were driven back, but a counterattack by Confederate brigadier general Clement A. Evans stopped the Union advance. Next, Pegram's and Major General William Mahone's divisions attacked the Union center near Dabney's Mill, south of Hatcher's Run. The Union line collapsed under the attack but re-formed north of the mill, parallel to Hatcher's Run. Confederate general Pegram was killed in the action. On February 7, Warren's men drove back the Confederates, recapturing most of the Union lines around Dabney's Mill. The Battle of Hatcher's Run saw the loss of 1,161 Confederates and 1,539 Union soldiers.

Thomas Jay Burgess, with his wife and sons, Lewis and Rush, had earlier moved to Dinwiddie County from New York, where he became interested in building the plank road from Petersburg to Boydton, Virginia. Burgess purchased a large plantation on Hatcher's Run from Mrs. Goodwyn, erecting a large gristmill and sawmill. These mills, together with all other buildings, were totally destroyed during the war, and the land was torn up and rendered almost valueless by forts and breastworks. It was here that the Battle of Hatcher's Run or Burgess Mill was fought. At the close of the war, Thomas's youngest son, Clark, would rebuild the place and attempt to restore it. His family spent their remaining years there. They were buried in the old Blandford Cemetery.

The Battle of Lewis's Farm (also known as Quaker Road, Military Road or Gravelly Road) was fought on March 29, 1865, in Dinwiddie County. It was the opening of the Appomattox Campaign, in which Confederate general Robert E. Lee's army was dislodged from their besieged lines around Petersburg, Virginia, and began to signal a retreat that would lead them to surrender at Appomattox Courthouse. On March 29, 1865, in the opening moves of Lieutenant General Ulysses S. Grant's spring offensive, Major General Philip Sheridan marched with the army's cavalry followed by the Fifth Corps toward Dinwiddie Courthouse to turn the right flank of General Robert E. Lee's Petersburg defenses. The Union's Fifth Corps under Major General Gouverneur K. Warren crossed Rowanty Creek, moved up Quaker Road toward the Boydton Plank Road intersection and encountered Major General Bushrod Johnson's Confederate brigades. A sharp firefight forced the Confederates back to their entrenchments on the White Oak Road. The remains of the Lewis farmhouse were burned on July 10, 2012 (it had fallen in on itself years go). A nearby highway marker still stands along Quaker Road.

The brigade of Brigadier General Joshua Chamberlain was obvious in the engagement, leading the main advance. Lieutenant General Richard H. Anderson ordered two brigades that had dug in to move forward to intercept Chamberlain, who, although shot from his horse, wounded (in the left arm and chest) and nearly captured, rallied his troops with the help of a four-gun battery. Reinforced, Chamberlain counterattacked and captured the enemy's earthworks. Colonel Alfred L. Pearson, in command of the 155th Pennsylvania Infantry, also known as "Pearson's Zouaves," would belatedly receive the Congressional Medal of Honor, thirty-two years after the Battle of Lewis's Farm. His citation reads: "At Lewis' Farm on March 29, 1865, seeing a brigade forced back by the enemy, he seized his regimental color, called on his men to follow him, and advanced upon the enemy under a severe fire. The whole brigade took up the advance, the lost ground was regained, and the enemy was repulsed. Date of issue: September 17, 1897." The Battle of Lewis's Farm saw the loss of 371 Confederates and 381 Union soldiers.

The Battle of Dinwiddie Courthouse was the foreword to the pivotal Battle of Five Forks. On March 29, 1865, the Cavalry Corps, along with the Second

Joshua Chamberlain achieved fame at the Battle of Gettysburg, where his valiant defense of a hill named Little Round Top became the focus of many publications and stories, including the novel *The Killer Angels* and the film *Gettysburg*. *Courtesy of the Library of Congress.*

and Fifth Corps of the Army of the Potomac, under Major General Philip Sheridan, attempted to flank General Robert E. Lee's Petersburg defenses. A heavy rain turned the clay and dirt roads quickly into knee-deep mud, slowing his advance. On March 31, Major General Rooney Lee's cavalry and Major General George Pickett's infantry division met the Union forces

Before Five Forks—Sheridan at Dinwiddie Court House. By James E. Taylor, 1839–1901. *Courtesy Smithsonian Institution, National Museum of American History: Archives Center*.

JAMES. E. TAYLOR
NY

just north and northwest of Dinwiddie Courthouse and drove them back, collapsing the Union lines into a snug line around the village of Dinwiddie. More Union infantry approached from the east, so George Pickett withdrew before daybreak to entrench at the road junction at Five Forks. Robert E. Lee then ordered George Pickett to hold this intersection at all costs. The Battle of Dinwiddie Courthouse saw the loss of 760 Confederates and 354 Union soldiers.

The Battle of White Oak Road occurred early on the morning of March 31, 1865. Confederate general Robert E. Lee sent most of a division forward to attack the Union forces from this location. Fighting through the morning, the Confederate brigades enveloped and put to flight two Union divisions in succession. Lewellyn Shaver, of the Sixtieth Alabama, was posted just to the west and wrote, "We were in line of battle in a piece of woods in front of which distant about 50 yards lay the road. Beyond…an extensive field, probably a mile and a half in length by a half mile in width. In this field, about a hundred and fifty yards from the road, was a line of picket holes, each fifty yards apart, occupied by Confederate riflemen." Beyond, Shaver noted, were "two heavy lines of battle of Union infantry, distinctly visible on the further edge of the field."

Four Confederate brigades formed in the woods on the north side of White Oak Road and then advanced into the Union columns. Brigadier General Romeyn B. Ayres's Union division was crushed under the onslaught and fled, along with Brigadier General Samuel Crawford's division, back across Gravelly Run to the south. A member of the Sixth Wisconsin recalled, "The formation of our lines was not completed before the enemy attacked us, bursting through gaps in our lines…catching the 3rd brigade while getting into position and driving them back in confusion, which exposed the right flank of our brigade and our regiment especially."

Confederate general Robert E. Lee rode along these fortifications on the morning of March 31 inspecting the lines to the cheering of his men. He learned from Bushrod Johnson's men that Union troops in front of the works had their "left flank in the air." To take advantage of this careless disposition of Union troops, Lee was determined to attack and to roll up the exposed Union flank. The Battle of White Oak Road saw the loss of 800 Confederates and 1,870 Union soldiers.

The Battle of Five Forks was fought on April 1, 1865, twelve miles southwest of Petersburg. The battle has sometimes been referred to as the "Waterloo of the Confederacy," and it pitted Union major general Philip H. Sheridan against Confederate major general George E. Pickett of Robert

A Currier & Ives lithograph entitled *The Battle of Petersburg, April 2nd 1865*—but it was an image of the fighting at the Battle of Five Forks. *Author's collection.*

E. Lee's Army of Northern Virginia. Pickett's loss at Five Forks triggered Lee's decision to abandon his entrenchments around Petersburg and begin the retreat that led to his surrender at Appomattox Courthouse on April 9. Sheridan's attack planned for Warren to advance in a two-division front with the third division following in reserve. The right front division, under Major General Samuel W. Crawford, was to strike at an angle near the end of the enemy's works, and the left front, under Major General Romeyn B. Ayres, was to strike the line head-on. But because of the poor intelligence, the flank was west of where Sheridan thought, so Crawford's division missed the line completely as it moved forward, and Ayres's men were subjected to enfilade fire from the left as they brushed past it.

The two Union divisions floundered in confusion as they frantically attempted to reorient themselves through the heavy thickets of underbrush. The reserve division, under Major General Charles Griffin, halted rather than add to the confusion. Warren, who chose to remain in a central location, sent all of his aides galloping off with messages to reorient the attack, but they were ineffective, so he rode out to take personal command.

As the Confederates attempted to organize a new defensive line, Griffin's division moved in on Ayres's right and attacked. Then Warren ordered

A dead South Carolina soldier in the trenches, April 1865. The soldier is wearing a gunner's haversack, which confirms his identity as an artilleryman. The photographer placed a broken gun sponge in the scene as a prop, which indicates that the image was taken to the rear of the battery. *Courtesy of the Library of Congress.*

Crawford's division to join the fight from the north. Sheridan's cavalry swept around Pickett's right flank but was unable to prevent several Confederates from escaping. However, it was a decisive Union victory, in which nearly a third of Pickett's 9,200 men were casualties. Given his losses at Gettysburg, this was a huge personal defeat for Pickett. The Battle of Five Forks saw the loss of 2,950 Confederates and 830 Union soldiers.

On April 2, 1865, Union forces commanded by Ulysses S. Grant attacked a portion of Robert E. Lee's army southwest of Petersburg. More than fourteen thousand Northern troops swarmed ahead in a pre-dawn attack, larger than Pickett's Charge at Gettysburg, and shattered Lee's line beyond repair. Known to history as "The Breakthrough," this engagement forced General Lee to advise the Confederate government in Richmond to evacuate

Battle of Five Forks Confederate prisoners of war. *Courtesy of the Library of Congress.*

the capital and ended the Petersburg Campaign, a military stalemate that had lasted more than nine months. Exactly one week after the breakthrough battle, Lee surrendered to Grant at Appomattox Courthouse.

The Battle of Sutherland's Station was fought on April 2, 1865, in Dinwiddie. Union forces converged on the city of Petersburg on April 2, pushing through a large section of the Confederate defensive entrenchments. As General Robert E. Lee desperately sought time to allow his army's withdraw, Ulysses S. Grant launched several other attacks. The Confederate forbearance at Fort Gregg helped delay Grant's progress. Meanwhile, Union major general Nelson A. Miles's division battered Henry Heath's Confederates at Sutherland's Station (Route 460) and drove them off the field. The Confederate defenders who remained were scattered and driven northwestward. The Union forces now possessed the South Side Railroad, General Robert E. Lee's last supply line into Petersburg. The defense of Fort Gregg and Grant's hesitation in aggressively following up on his success at Sutherland's Station permitted Lee's army to evacuate that night, heading toward Sailors Creek and later the village of Appomattox.

Left: Confederate general Ambrose P. Hill was killed April 2, 1865. Hill, not knowing that Lee's lines had been broken, rode into a party of Union soldiers advancing on Petersburg. *Courtesy of the Library of Congress.*

Below: Alexander Gardner's photo. General John Gibbon transporting captured colors of the Army of Northern Virginia to Washington, May 1, 1865. Here General John Gibbon and Medal of Honor winners prepare to present the captured colors of the Army of Northern Virginia at Fort Gregg to Secretary of War Edwin M. Stanton. *Courtesy of a private collector.*

In his groundbreaking book *The Confederate Alamo: Bloodbath at Petersburg's Fort on April 2, 1865*, John J. Fox wrote of the battle at Dinwiddie's Fort Gregg. Robert E. Lee faced the most monumental crisis of his military career that morning, as by sunrise that day, the Union Sixth Corps had punched a huge hole in Lee's outer line, southwest of Petersburg. Lee needed time for reinforcements to arrive from Richmond, but how could his depleted army buy that time? Against overwhelming odds, a handful of Confederates made a desperate last stand at Fort Gregg, an action that could only be described as a suicide mission.

Famous historian Douglas Southall Freeman called this epic fight "one of the most dramatic incidents of an overwhelming day," and yet it has been overshadowed by all the other historic events of April 1865. Fourteen Union soldiers received the Medal of Honor for their bravery at Fort Gregg. Many battle-scarred veterans from both sides described this clash as the nastiest of their four-year war experience. At 1:00 p.m. on April 2, 1865, the initial assault by Union forces began on nearby Fort Gregg by Major General John Gibbon's Twenty-fourth Corps. "Men, the salvation of Lee's army is in your keeping," Major General Cadmus Wilcox told the defenders of Fort Gregg that day as five thousand Union forces swept forward to attack Fort Gregg. The mere three hundred Confederates twice drove the Union forces back, but finally the attackers reached the fort's parapet. For twenty minutes, a vicious hand-to-hand battle raged on.

At fight's end, the fort belonged to the Union forces. Only forty-four Confederates survived the battle, most badly wounded. A sixteen-year-old Dinwiddie Rebel named Homer Atkinson (a private of Captain Wolf's company, Virginia Second Class Militia) was still standing inside Fort Gregg. Once in the prisoner line, a Union colonel said, "Is it possible the South has gotten to that point of using children as you are, for soldiers?" This officer then pulled the boy aside, preventing him from being sent to the prison boat at City Point. He remained behind and was paroled on April 19. Atkinson would later serve as the chief officer of the Military Order of Stars and Bars from its beginning until his death in 1945. In addition to commanding the new order, Captain Atkinson also served two terms as commander-in-chief of the United Confederate Veterans. The two hours gained by Fort Gregg's defenders allowed Lee to evacuate Petersburg safely that night. With the fall of Fort Gregg and nearby Fort Whitworth, Lee's Confederates pulled back to their last, innermost line.

Nearby, the Battle of Fort Whitworth—also known as Fort Baldwin, Alexander or Anderson—was garrisoned by the Nineteenth and Forty-eighth Mississippi Infantry of Brigadier General Nathaniel Harris's brigade. This battery was initially supported by guns of Louisiana's Washington Artillery, but these were withdrawn from the fort during the battle. Eventually, Fort Whitworth was attacked by Brigadier General Thomas M. Harris's West Virginia brigade (Tenth, Eleventh and Fifteenth Regiments). With the subsequent capture of Fort Gregg by the Union forces, General Lee ordered Whitworth evacuated, forcing his troops to fall back into the city defenses.

Judge David Meade Bernard was born in Petersburg on May 11, 1840. His parents were Virginians—his father, David Meade Bernard Sr., was born in King George County, and his mother, Sallie A. Field, was born in Brunswick County. His marriage was solemnized in Brunswick County on December 21, 1870, by Reverends J.H. Morrison and O.A. Glazebrook, and his wife, Lutie B., was the daughter of Dr. Edward A. Morrison. The children of Judge and Mrs. Bernard are Lutie M., Sallie F., Mary M., Willie M., David M. and Richard F. Judge Bernard went to school in Petersburg until 1857 and then was sent to Hampden-Sydney College, where he graduated in 1860. He entered the Confederate States Army in May 1851; served as a private in Company K, Twelfth Virginia Infantry; was transferred to Tenth Virginia Cavalry in 1864, where he served through the war; was wounded on March 31, 1865, near Dinwiddie Courthouse; and was captured at Richmond, at the time of the evacuation. After the war, he returned to his home in Orange, studied law and was admitted to the bar in Brunswick County in May 1866. He practiced there and in adjoining counties until 1881. At this time, he moved to Petersburg, where he was in practice until January 1886, when he became judge of the Husting's Court of Petersburg.

William E. Beasley was born in Petersburg on June 4, 1842. He went to school at the Petersburg Institute and in 1859 engaged with his father in the tobacco business. He entered the Confederate army in April 1861, serving as a lieutenant in Company D, Twelfth Virginia Infantry. In 1862, he resigned and later reenlisted, this time in the cavalry service of Company B, Thirteenth Virginia Regiment. After the war, he went to Louisville, Kentucky, and was in the tobacco business there for a year, then he returned to Petersburg, where he continued in the same business. His father, William H. Beasley, was born in Petersburg and died in July 1874 at age sixty-three. His wife, whom he married March 25, 1864, was Mary J. Hill, born in Dinwiddie County, the daughter of Green Hill, who died in 1865 at age sixty. Her mother was Mary Eldredge, a descendant of Pocahontas.

The sorrowful inscription of a mother's note, a lock of her son's hair and a childhood image are a testament to the cost of war. "My beloved son Carl taken from me on April 1, 1865, at age 18, killed at Dinwiddie. Flights of angels sing thee to thy rest." A quote from *Hamlet*, Act 5, Scene 2. He's probably Carlos E. Rogers, 185th New York, killed March 29–30, 1865, at Quaker Road. *Courtesy of the Library of Congress.*

Civil War Congressional Medal of Honor recipient Henry M. Hardenbergh served as a private in the Union army in Company G, Thirty-ninth Illinois Infantry. He was awarded the Medal of Honor for action on August 16, 1864, at Deep Run, Virginia. His citation reads: "Capture of flag. He was wounded in the shoulder during this action. He was killed in action at Petersburg on August 28, 1864" and is buried in Poplar Grove National Cemetery, Dinwiddie County.

Civil War Congressional Medal of Honor recipient Sergeant Lewis Morgan was born in 1836 in Delaware County, Ohio. He served in Company I, Fourth Ohio Infantry, Union army. In actions with the Confederate general Robert E. Lee's forces at Spotsylvania Courthouse on May 12, 1864, Sergeant Morgan captured the flag from the enemy's works. He was later killed at the Battle of Hatcher's Run during the Siege of Petersburg and posthumously awarded the Medal of Honor on December 1, 1864. He died on October 27, 1864, and was buried in the Poplar Grove National Cemetery, Dinwiddie County.

Frederick William Benteen, a Union soldier, was born August 24, 1834, in Petersburg. From 1861 to 1865, he was a colonel in the United States volunteers, and he served gallantly in numerous battles and skirmishes. He was a brigadier general of the Missouri militia, and he was brevetted a brigadier general of the United States Army. He resided in Atlanta, Georgia, where he was prominent in the business and public affairs of that city. He died about 1898 in Atlanta.

The previous individuals are just a mere sampling of the thousands who fought and died in Dinwiddie County during the American Civil War. One of those was the ancestral cousin of the author, Captain Henry Seagrave, who led his company, the Thirtieth United States Colored Troops, at the Battle of the Crater. He was left for dead on the field, taken prisoner, brought to Petersburg and then sent to Libby Prison, where he was made part of a prisoner exchange and sent home to Uxbridge, Massachusetts. Unfortunately, he died shortly thereafter from his wounds.

In the aftermath of the Civil War, martial law continued over Virginia for the next decade. From 1861, martial law had been proclaimed, and legal rights were denied in both civil and military court as the Union army seized control of Virginia. Public buildings and streets fell into disrepair, schools and churches closed and one-third of the city's houses were seized. Supplies dwindled, and the economy of Virginia started to collapse. All too quickly, profiteers crowded Virginia. The *Petersburg Index* newspaper on July 4, 1865, reported the following robbery: "There was stolen from the Southside depot Sunday night, 10 cases

The Fiftieth New York Volunteer Engineers originally occupied the Flower Farm prior to the creation of the Poplar Grove Cemetery in 1865. There they constructed the loblolly pine Gothic-style chapel that existed through 1869, when reburials ended. *Courtesy of the Library of Congress.*

of liquor, and each case containing 12 bottles. Somebody is going to enjoy the Fourth." Then on July 6, 1865, it was reported:

> *Some creature without the fear of Providence or Provost Marshals broke into the pastor study of the First Baptist Church on Saturday night last, by breaking through one of the windows, and stole several valuable articles*

of clothing belonging to the Rev. Thomas Hume, Jr., who is temporarily filling the pulpit of the church. No clue has as yet been discovered as to the perpetrators of this crime. Anyone who is so far debased as to steal from the House of God, is too despicable to be classed among rational beings and we know that were he transformed into a Beast, Bird or Fish, that a meeting would be held by these creatures and the disgraceful puppy (we ask our pardon dogs!) be kicked out of their domains, and sent to some quadruped Tophet out of which there is no redemption.

This was followed on July 7, 1865, by the news of a fatal affray: "Yesterday evening, about seven o'clock, a difficulty occurred between a soldier and a [black] man, near Butterworth's bridge, resulting in a most serious wound to the soldier. Our informant thinks that death must ensue. The late news of the hour prevented particulars in detail—They will appear in our next issue. The blow was given with an axe. The Provost Marshall sent a sufficient force to the spot to preserve order and arrest the black man."

Since Dinwiddie women were not allowed to fight for their Southern homeland, they sought a way to show their patriotic passion. They did this by sewing a bright blue banner to be carried by the Dinwiddie men who did fight. The flag is currently on display at Pamplin Historical Park.

In July 1861, volunteers with the Dinwiddie Cavalry became Company K, Third Virginia Cavalry Regiment, of the Confederate States of America. They were sent to protect the Tidewater Peninsula from the Union forces, and they took their banner with them. It bore the state seal of Virginia on the back and, on the front, the inscription "Presented by the Ladies of Dinwiddie County, VA." But a year later, in retreat after a skirmish with Union forces near Williamsburg, their precious flag was captured. For nearly eighty years after that, it was kept by the family of the late Colonel David Campbell, of the Fifth Pennsylvania Cavalry. The Campbells finally sent it back to Dinwiddie in 1941. From then until 1998, the flag was displayed at the Dinwiddie Clerk's Office and then the Historic Fork Inn in Sutherland. Along the way, light, air and humidity drained away its color and damaged the fragile silk fibers. It was on a slow course to oblivion, but it is now safely on display at Pamplin Historical Park.

The *Petersburg Index* of July 20, 1865, reported one of the most disturbing postwar incidents, a fatal affray:

Last evening about 4 o'clock a Negro named William Stewart was shot and killed instantly by a guard named Adolph Schempe Co B 41st NY.

Dinwiddie County's battle flag. *Courtesy of Pamplin Historical Park.*

> *From all that we can learn it seems that this boy was being carried down Old street, under arrest and when he neared Sycamore street he endeavored to get away from the guard in order to get to his place of business, as he was engaged as a cook by Rennache & Brothers, who kept a store under the library building on Sycamore street. He endeavored to wrest the gun from the hands of the guard by seizing it in both hands and as he was much stronger than the guard he succeeded in pulling him some distance across the street when seeing some of the guards from the guard house across the street, approaching to the assistance of Schempe the negro loosened his hold and ran when the guard first attempted to stick him with the bayonet and not succeeding, he shot him, the ball entering one side of his head and coming out on the other killing him instantly. The guard was placed under arrest we believe.*

Among the more than 6,100 Union graves in Dinwiddie County's Poplar Grove National Cemetery is that of William Montgomery, a member of the 155th Pennsylvania who holds the unfortunate distinction of being the last

The annual lighting of luminaries at Poplar Grove National Cemetery in commemoration of Veterans Day draws dozens of volunteers, including Boy Scout and Girl Scout troops, to place white paper bags containing candles on each grave marker at the 147-year-old cemetery off Vaughan Road. *Author's collection.*

enlisted man killed in Virginia in the Civil War. He would be very far from being the last American to fall in the service of his country, however.

Every November, National Park Service rangers, volunteers and area residents light candles on Montgomery's final resting place and all the others at Poplar Grove in tribute to those soldiers and all the other men and women who have served in the nation's armed forces.

As twilight falls, the soft glow of the candles emerges in long, neat, curving lines stretching across the grounds, in a solemn act of continued gratitude for the nation's defenders. The names of more than four thousand of the soldiers buried at Poplar Grove are unknown. Visitors to the Petersburg National Battlefield visitor center recently were offered the opportunity to write names on the bags used for the ceremony, personal tributes to their ancestors or loved ones who served or are serving in the military. As a result, there were reminders of every war America has fought, from "John Lumsden, Virginia Militia, Revolutionary War" to "Cpl. Ben Kopp, Army Ranger, died from wounds in Afghanistan, donated his organs so others could live, True American Hero." And this testimony to new tragedy closer to home: "Pvt. Francheska Velez, Ft. Hood, TX, 5 Nov. 09. Love, Papo."

At one such ceremony at William Montgomery's grave, park ranger Tyler Wilson stood in torchlight wearing the flamboyant Zouave uniform of the 155th Pennsylvania as he told visitors the details of Montgomery's death. Near Appomattox Courthouse, he "received a mortal wound from shrapnel from a Confederate battery that was retreating" on the very day Lee surrendered to Grant. Other National Park rangers explained how fallen soldiers' bodies were collected for interment during the Civil War, why so many of those buried at Poplar Grave are unknown and that among the graves there are more than three hundred soldiers of the United States Colored Troops.

Chapter 6

RECONSTRUCTION AND GROWTH

1866–1916

Dinwiddie's population continued to grow throughout the nineteenth century. In 1880, it stood at 13,017, up from about 5,257 in 1830. The number of black citizens outnumbered the white population by 4,647. There were a total of fifteen rural post offices, nine churches of various faiths, forty-one stores and nine gristmills in the county. Two hotels were open, one at the courthouse and one at Reams Station. The population of the village of Dinwiddie Courthouse was 75.

The end of slavery meant the relocation of the many former slaves. Some remained in the area in various private houses. While few houses remain from the early days of freedom, the many small hamlets settled by the former slaves still survive throughout the county. A good example is found in the southern tier of the county at Masontown, located east of McKenney, where a well-preserved academic building, the Masontown School, survives. Many former slaves continued to work for their former masters or their successors. The end of the Confederacy spelled ruin to most of the county's old families and large landowners.

Joseph P. Evans was born a slave in 1835 in Dinwiddie County and purchased his freedom in 1859. During Reconstruction, he was a prominent leader of Petersburg's African American community, serving as a delegate to the Republican state convention of 1867 and in the Virginia House of Delegates from 1871 to 1873, representing Petersburg. Mr. Evans also served in the Senate of Virginia from 1874 to 1875. While a member of the General Assembly, Mr. Evans introduced bills to require compulsory education, to guarantee African Americans the right to serve on juries and to require landlords to give ten days' notice before evicting tenants. He also held positions as a letter carrier and as deputy collector of internal revenue. He was elected president of a black labor convention in Richmond in 1875, where he urged African Americans to organize themselves independently in politics and as workers. He ran unsuccessfully as an independent candidate for Congress in 1884. His son, William Evans, represented Petersburg in the General Assembly from 1887 to 1888. Joseph P. Evans died in 1888.

Thomas Lipton was just seventeen when he arrived in New York from England and took a job as a former slave on the Samuel Clay plantation near Wilsons Depot, which today is a small village off Route 460 in Dinwiddie County, though it was formerly a railroad and water stop. It was always believed that Lipton left no written records about the nine months he worked on the Clay farm from the summer of 1866 until early 1867, when a leg injury forced him to leave the job. Then, Emporia resident Terry Botts showed me in 2010 "a historical sensation." Behind a glass frame, Botts keeps a three-page letter dated February 24, 1926, that Lipton sent Ambler Brook Moncure, who resided on Old Stage Road in Dinwiddie County at the time. Lipton went on to describe his experience: "I was engaged in New York to go to work for Sam Clay near Wilson's Depot in Dinwiddie County, and on first arriving at the estate, I slept in a little hut, but my boss, Mr. Sam Clay, apparently thought so well of me that he afterwards took me into his big house." Note that Lipton used a slave's term—"big house"—in describing Clay's residence. Clay had three sons, though Lipton referred to only Robert and Travis in his letter. Patrick, the oldest son, had established himself as a farmer. Lipton also talked about Clay's daughters. "[Clay] had two young daughters, who treated me most kindly and made me feel quite at home." He then wrote about his travels to Charleston and New Orleans. Then Lipton stated, "The goal of my life, however, was to make money for the old folks at home, and when I had saved what I thought was sufficient I came home and open my first little shop, bring with me a barrel of flour and rocking chair for my mother."

Lipton gained much more than money during his early travels in America, because he witnessed international trade and commerce firsthand and later applied those concepts to the foundation of his own tea empire, which would become one of the most successful businesses of its kind in the world. Today, Lipton Tea owns about 10 percent of the world's tea market, and the famous Lipton Iced Tea is available in more than sixty countries. Moncure, the

Sir Thomas Lipton. *Author's collection.*

Olive Branch Baptist Church was organized in 1868. *Photo by author.*

letter's recipient, responded on March 17, 1926, and invited Lipton to stay at his house in Wilsons, should he ever come back to visit Dinwiddie County. "Oh what pleasure it gave me to know that the Clay's upheld the tradition of this old state by showing courtesy and kindness to a stranger among them," he wrote.

William W. Evans was born a slave in 1860 in Dinwiddie County. The son of Joseph P. and Josephine Evans, William Evans began his working career as a barber but ended as a self-made lawyer. He attended school in Petersburg and purchased real estate. He represented Petersburg in the Virginia House of Delegates from 1887 to 1888.

The Freedmen's Bureau established new facilities for freedmen, including a mental health hospital in December 1869 at Howard's Grove Hospital, a former Confederate unit. In 1870, the General Assembly incorporated the Central Lunatic Asylum as an organized state institution as part of an effort by the Reconstruction-era legislature to increase public institutions for general welfare. The legislature also founded the state's first system of free public education. Central State Hospital opened in 1885 in Dinwiddie County first as a segregated facility for mentally ill African Americans, and the hospital's chapel and Amusement Hall were built in 1904. The building was used for social activities, as well as daily and Sunday worship services. Central State Hospital is now being phased out of operation.

The Church of the Good Shepherd was established in 1887 on Lew Jones Road. *Photo by author.*

In 1882, the Commonwealth of Virginia passed a bill sponsored by Alfred W. Harris, a black lawyer and Howard University graduate from Petersburg. As an elected state representative from Dinwiddie County, Harris proposed that the state charter a normal college for the purpose of educating its black citizens. Although a lengthy lawsuit against the school delayed its opening as opponents of black education in the state tried to block its establishment, the Virginia Normal and Collegiate Institute welcomed 126 students to classes in October 1883. Black statesman and lawyer John Mercer Langston became its first president. The school was housed in an enormous multi-story, multi-sectional building designed by Harrison Wait, and it became a Petersburg landmark. In 1902, the state legislature voted to curtail the collegiate program and accordingly renamed the school the Virginia Normal and Industrial Institute. The land grant program originally housed at Hampton Institute relocated to Virginia Normal in 1920, which helped to reinstate the collegiate program in 1923. In 1930, the school's name was changed to Virginia State College for Negroes, then to Virginia State College in 1946 and finally Virginia State University in 1979. From the 1920s onward, the school rejected the Tuskegee model of industrial education, which denigrated academic excellence, and strove instead for quality education in the liberal arts and sciences. The school currently enrolls over 4,300 students.

Ellis Wilson, a farmer and minister, was born a slave in 1824. He spent his entire life in Dinwiddie County as a minister and community leader. In 1870 and 1871, he purchased 624 acres. He represented Dinwiddie County in the Virginia House of Delegates from 1869 to 1871. It is believed that Mr. Wilson died in 1904.

R.D. Ruffin, a lawyer, was born a slave in 1837 in King and Queen County. Mr. Ruffin fought in the American Civil War and became a sergeant. He studied law at Howard University and graduated in 1874. After graduation, he first settled in Alexandria but later moved to Dinwiddie County to practice law and enter politics. He represented Dinwiddie County in the Virginia House of Delegates from 1875 to 1876 and served as the sheriff of Alexandria County from 1873 to 1874.

Darvill's School, a public school, operated in the western corner of the county as early as the 1880s. In 1907, three other one-room schools nearby were consolidated here as Darvills Graded School, which was expanded and made into a high school in 1913. It was the heart of community activities, notably the annual Darvills Fair, which began in 1916 and continued through the 1930s. The school closed in 1942, and its buildings were razed, except for the original graded school, which became a community center. It burned on July 5, 1998.

The Central State Hospital Kitchen operation in the early 1900s. *Courtesy of Petersburg Museums.*

In this 1901 photograph, Laura Watkins wears a dress and hat made by Bettie Ford Watkins, Laura's mother. *Courtesy of the Watkins family.*

1909 United Confederate Veterans Reunion on the steps of the Siege Museum of Petersburg. Homer Atkinson, Past Commander, #2 front row right, was captured at Fort Gregg, in Dinwiddie County, on April 2, 1865, at age sixteen. *Courtesy of Petersburg Museum.*

In 1904, the Confederate Veterans Camp #18, "J.E.B. Stuart, No. 1"—Commander Charles E. Abernathy and Adjutant A.M. Orgain Jr.—was meeting at the Dinwiddie Courthouse.

Chapter 7

WORLD WAR I TO WORLD WAR II

1917–1945

The World War I draft board for Dinwiddie County and Petersburg was composed of the following members: Nelson T. Patterson; Honorable Thomas E. Clarke; W.H. Creckford, MD, who was succeeded by R.A. Martin, MD, who served June 1917 to August 2, 1917; and its chief clerk was H.D. Atkinson. The board was headquartered in Petersburg. Hundreds of Diwiddians were called up or enlisted, and many died. The following group of individuals all gave their lives: Sterling Booth, Joseph Henry Johnson, Buddie Rose, Sam Crittenden, Junious Johnson, Willie Short, Walter Hayes, Ruffin Jones, Lewis Morton Wimbush and Isaac Robinson. They were black men who fought in a clearly segregated army. They may have been fighting for more than the defense of Europe and America, possibly for the hope of equal rights. The white men who gave their lives included Lyman H. Green, Maurice E. Olgers, Webster W. Thompson, Walter S. Hardy, William Berkeley Peebles, Benjamin E. Wells, Charles W. Lewis, O'Ferral N. Suiter, Thomas D. Wells, Macy Maitland and Samuel W. Temple.

Dinwiddie's population declined significantly in the twentieth century. Farming remained the county's principal source of employment and economic sustenance during the period between the World Wars. The town of McKenney was issued its charter of incorporation on March 22, 1922. Commerce continued to focus on buildings on contiguous lots in McKenney and around Dinwiddie Courthouse and on small villages and hamlets like Sutherland, Carson, Ford and Dewitt. Dwellings were built on the periphery. New buildings replaced old buildings or were added on to existing structures.

A new bank was built opposite the Dinwiddie Courthouse, a two-story brick structure called the Planter's Bank. It was then an imposing addition to the county seat.

Compared to the period of slow agricultural change and stable population that followed the Civil War, the period following World War I was one of increasing change. The population of the county seat increased very modestly as the twentieth century progressed. Government, service and commercial activities remained the county seat's principal source of employment and growth during the period between the world wars.

There were no county planning or zoning ordinances during this period. The federal census population between 1940 and 1950 for Dinwiddie County showed limited growth. The Great Depression did not seriously affect rural Dinwiddie as it did larger communities with an industrial labor base, but land values and prices for agricultural products were very low, and historic buildings suffered as maintenance was deferred. Life in general was hard. Cultivation of less productive land was abandoned, and it was allowed to revert to timber. Large historic houses, such as Darvills and Denmark, were allowed to deteriorate. The historic agricultural landscapes that had characterized Dinwiddie since the eighteenth century showed signs of unraveling, as the roadsides began to crowd with houses and crossroads sprouted new commercial ventures.

Historic resources, such as early service stations, once were at many prominent rural locations across the county. Among the most interesting of these sites is the Jamerson's Service Station, circa 1920. It's an example of a commercial building dating from the interwar period. Although relocated a short distance from its original site, it retains many original features. According to the owners, it was operated by a man named Mayhew. The building later became a transmission repair shop operated by Mayhew and Jamerson. The building is a one-story frame with a central chimney and six-over-six sash windows, with a large shop window flanking the central entry. The hipped metal roof extends to form a canopy to protect gas pumps; a sign on the canopy indicates that the building is Jamerson's Service Station.

Fitz Lee was a Buffalo Soldier in the United States Army and a recipient of America's highest military decoration, the Medal of Honor, for his actions in the Spanish-American War. Lee joined the army from his birth place of Dinwiddie County, and by June 30, 1898, he was serving as a private in Troop M of the Tenth Cavalry Regiment. On that day, American forces aboard the USS *Florida* near Tayacoba, Cuba, dispatched a small landing party to provide reconnaissance on Spanish outposts in the area.

Planter's Bank. *Photo by author.*

In 1933, Billy Wingfield and Chatton Harmon walked to school barefoot. *Courtesy of the Watkins family*.

They were discovered by Spanish scouts and came under heavy cannon fire; their boats were sunk, thus stranding them on shore. The *Florida* launched several rescue attempts; the first four were forced to retreat under heavy fire. The fifth attempt, manned by Lee and three other privates of the Tenth Cavalry, launched at night and successfully found and rescued the surviving members of the original landing party. One year later, on June 23, 1899, all four rescuers were awarded the Medal of Honor for their actions in what had come to be known as the Battle of Tayacoba. Fitz Lee died shortly after receiving the medal; he was buried in Fort Leavenworth National Cemetery, Leavenworth County, Kansas.

As war loomed in mid-December 1941, the return of the 1861 Dinwiddie Cavalry flag occurred. It was returned from "friends in the North to the spot where it first floated high," Virginia state senator Henry T. Wickham announced. He would go on to say, "Recall to us Oh! Spirit, some of your glorious memories from the day when you first saw the light from the eyes of the noble women who made you, and presented you to this gallant company on the very spot we now stand." This flag is now gratefully maintained by Virginia Historical Society and may be seen by appointment.

In late 1941, as war drew closer to America's shores, United States Army surveyors visited the site of a former Civilian Conservation Corps camp near the small rural town of Blackstone, Virginia, on the outskirts of Dinwiddie County. There they found enough land, water and other resources needed to establish a post large enough to simultaneously train more than one infantry division. The site also offered easy railroad access to both mountain and coastal training sites. By December 1941, nearly forty-six thousand acres of land in Nottoway, Dinwiddie, Lunenburg and Brunswick Counties were acquired and cleared to establish Camp Pickett.

Units of the Virginia National Guard had their first use of what is now Camp Pickett on December 6–7 when the First Battalion, 116th Infantry, camped there, having just completed a series of war games in North Carolina. The rapid development of Fort Pickett became a top priority after the United States' entry in World War II. Two rail spurs were built to the camp in 1942–43 to increase logistical efficiency and the rapid movement of troops. Air transportation to and from Camp Pickett started with the completion of a four-runway airfield in late 1942. The runways were large enough to safely land a Douglas C-47 "Gooney Bird." Even fighter planes could use the runway in an emergency, though none was stationed at the airfield. Aircraft fuel was delivered by rail and contained in fuel trucks. At the end of 1942, more than 1,400 buildings had been completed, including 1,000 enlisted

The Petersburg-Dinwiddie Airport was in full operation during World War II. *Courtesy of Petersburg Museum.*

barracks and 70 officers' quarters, 12 chapels, a hospital complex and 6 firehouses, along with warehouses and headquarters buildings. The army had to build and maintain its own water-pumping, filtration and sewage treatment plants for its potential sixty-thousand-soldier population. By war's end, more than 300 additional buildings were constructed, including barracks for women and facilities for two prisoner-of-war camps.

Camp Pickett seemed destined to close once again, but the demands of the Cold War and the need to train division-sized Reserve Component units in the mid-Atlantic region brought a new role for the fort. By 1960, portions were being revamped to house battalions coming for a week or two each year to conduct specialized training. This included not only guard/reserve commands but also marine corps and navy personnel. These units still use Pickett's facilities today under Virginia National Guard control.

The predecessor to the Virginia National Guard Maneuver Training Center was organized and stationed at Pickett in 1961. Its primary mission was to store and maintain pieces of equipment, such as tanks and other armored vehicles, that visiting units could use, rather than incurring the high cost of bringing their own machines from their home stations.

Pickett experienced two significant interrelated events in 1974 that marked its future path. The first was its re-designation from Camp Pickett to Fort Pickett, in a reflection of its new mission to offer quality training opportunities not only to reserve units but also active duty forces on a yearly basis. The second important event was the completion, for the first time since the Korean War, of a new building on post. Building 467 contained space not only to house enlisted personnel but also to serve as a mess facility and administrative area. More significantly, it was built of brick and intended as the first permanent structure in Pickett's history. In the 1980s, the army transferred control and operation of these facilities to the town of Blackstone. For recreation, there were four movie theaters, a fieldhouse with a gym, several enlisted clubs, a main post exchange (PX) and several "satellite" PXs.

Ten years later, new barracks and support structures were completed, large enough to house an entire brigade, all dedicated in memory of Technical Sergeant Frank D. Peregory of the 116th Infantry, on June 8, 1984, forty years to the day after he earned the Medal of Honor during the D-Day invasion. Later upgrades to runways would allow the use of C-130 and C-17 transport aircraft for access by airmobile troops and equipment coming via air to Fort Pickett for training.

Fort Pickett is the home of an annual exercise with elements of the Canadian Thirty-sixth Brigade Group, located in Nova Scotia and Prince Edward Island, Canada. Exercise South Bound Trooper is a joint exercise between the Canadian Forces Primary Reserves and Virginia National Guard that helps forge solid NATO doctrine between the two militaries. While the facilities at Pickett are geared to train military personnel and units, non-military organizations use them too. These sometimes include the U.S. Marshal's Service, Federal Bureau of Investigation, the Bureau of Alcohol, Tobacco, Firearms and Explosives (ATF), Civil Air Patrol, Virginia State Police and local law enforcement agencies. The decision to inactivate the regular army garrison at Fort Pickett and turn over operation of the post to the Virginia National Guard was enacted in 1997. Since then, no regular army personnel have been assigned to Pickett.

In 1943, the Petersburg-Dinwiddie Airport was converted from an emergency landing strip to an air delivery unit. When the workers arrived in Dinwiddie County, the airport had one tree-lined runway, no roads, no lights, no buildings, no telephones and no restrooms. There was a hotel nearby on

U.S. Route 1 called the Blue Tartan where the men stayed while working on the airport. Using equipment and army prisoners from Fort Lee, the airport was up and running in just three months. The new airport had three barracks, fuel storage, fueling trucks, maintenance facilities, a Red Cross canteen and restrooms. Pilots who flew in could stay at the Petersburg Hotel, in town, where the management arranged dances also attended by the local girls. Pilots would fly in from Brooklyn, New York, land at Petersburg and then head west. During the winter months, they flew from Dinwiddie to Atlanta, Texas and then on to the West Coast so that the planes could be sent to the Pacific theater. They then made the return trip with battle-worn planes needing repair. The Second World War was fought in too many locations for any serious accounting. By the war's end, Dinwiddie County would see the loss of one hundred of its noblest sons, and many others would come home suffering from long-term wounds. Today, the Dinwiddie Airport is a commercial airfield with two runways and a small modern terminal and is located off I-85 and Route 460.

Appomattox Riverside Park today is a sprawling 137 acres along electric lines and the remains of the former historic boat canal on the Appomattox River. This unique park, which was the former Ferndale Park, has views of the river's rapids, a large pavilion, office space, bathroom facilities and several smaller pavilions. Ferndale also once included a theater, merry-go-round with hobby horses and swings, and it offered refreshments, dances and bands. It was ten minutes by streetcar from downtown Petersburg.

This park is located along Ferndale Road in the northern end of Dinwiddie County, but it isn't a Dinwiddie County park. It's a City of Petersburg park encapsulated within the county. Before the land became a city park, it was the property of what is now Dominion Virginia Power. How the land became the property of Petersburg instead of the county is a bit of a mystery. However, this quirk could change as county officials have gone into preliminary talks about possibly taking ownership at the time this book was written.

In the late 1890s, William R. McKenney, an attorney for the Richmond, Petersburg and Carolina Railroad, set his sights on a parcel of land eleven miles southwest of Dinwiddie Courthouse, next to the San Marino Post Office. He succeeded in having the railroad establish a water stop in this community, and the town was named after him. It was Christmas of 1900 when the first steam train rumbled through the town of McKenney.

The emerging settlement revolved around its freight and passenger trains and a prosperous lumber industry. McKenney bustled with commercial activity, including the Bank of McKenney, first chartered as the Bank of

This is the former shooting gallery at Ferndale Park. On July 7, 1928, Edward Skinner was shot here with a .22-caliber rifle that was being loaded by Bolling Traylor. Frank Pond rushed him to the Petersburg hospital over ten miles away, but he died. *Author's collection.*

A rare German published postcard shows Jim Seay's bateau carrying people across the river, from Chesterfield County to Ferndale Park, in Dinwiddie County. Even in the 1920s, people were unsure where they were. James (Jim) Seay and his wife, Carrie, are buried in East Matoaca Cemetery. He was the last bateau man on the Dinwiddie County canal. *Author's collection.*

The Seaboard Air Line's *Southern States Special* rolls past the McKenney Train Station in 1947, heaed for New York. *Courtesy Bank of McKenney.*

Dinwiddie, which was established on June 5, 1906, with $10,000 in stock. The bank surpassed the odds and continued to grow even during the Depression, when many banks shut down.

Sallie Jones Atkinson, prominent educator and community leader in Dinwiddie County, and her husband, John Pryor Atkinson, gave the land on which Sunnyside High School was built in 1911. By her vision, tireless industry and determination, the school became the first eight-month rural school accredited in Virginia. Mrs. Atkinson also served on the state committee that worked to secure Governor Montague's approval for women's suffrage.

Chapter 8

THE NEW DOMINION

1946–PRESENT

The lumberman says, "I would like to buy your farm." The farmer says: "What is this, some kind of joke?" Many good stories begin with two men at a bar. *Lucy v. Zehmer*, which would become "a staple of contracts casebooks since shortly after it was decided" in 1954, is no exception. As now generations of law students have learned, the case of *Lucy v. Zehmer* involves two men talking over a bottle of liquor the weekend before Christmas at Ye Olde Virginnie, on U.S. Route 1 in McKenney. Adrian Hardy Zehmer, allegedly drunk and joking, scribbled a contract for the sale of a farm he owned on the back of a dinner receipt. Welford Ordway Lucy accepted and left, insisting that Zehmer was bound to the sale. The Virginia Supreme Court of Appeals ultimately agreed with Lucy, ruling that a signed contract, even one signed by two men drinking at a bar, is no laughing matter.

Five decades after Justice Buchanan issued his opinion in *Lucy v. Zehmer*, a law professor at the University of North Carolina in Chapel Hill prepared to discuss the case with his contracts class. Surveying the class to select a student to summarize the facts of the case, one name caught his eye. "Mr. Lucy, would you care to share what you know about this case?" That student was John C. Lucy IV, the great-grandson of the original co-plaintiff, John C. Lucy. Once again, a Lucy was being asked to explain the curious events in a Dinwiddie restaurant just days before Christmas in 1952. Over that half a century, much has changed in Dinwiddie County. The development of Interstate Highways 85 and 95, for example, has had a devastating effect on local businesses along Highway 1. A drive through the area reveals a virtual

McKenney Women's Club. The club of 1949 broke ground for a project to clean up an area of McKenney to build a playground for the neighboring children. *Front row, left to right:* Sarah Keesler, Olive Rives, Mary Bruce Butte, Lena Roberts, Elizabeth Hart and Everett Roberts. *Courtesy Bank of McKenney.*

rust belt of old hotels and restaurants nearly identical to Zehmer's place, Ye Olde Virginnie. As visitors will quickly realize, even Ye Olde Virginnie is no longer open to those passing through town; instead, in an ironic twist, Ye Olde Virginnie has been transformed into somewhat of a retirement community. Many of these changes began with the transformation of Virginia's economy in the 1950s and 1960s. Leading the way was Governor Albertis Harrison, who is fondly remembered as a driving force behind the modernization of industry across the state.

Regional prices for timber eventually stabilized, and large entities emerged to manage and harvest timberlands more efficiently than their family-owned predecessors. Perhaps one other thing to change will be the way law students will understand *Lucy v. Zehmer*. Unlike the caricature often portrayed in the contracts classroom, the case involves sophisticated businessmen, a tumultuous economic climate and the persistent lesson that appellate courts—and generations of contracts scholars—should be hesitant before stridently claiming to understand the facts of the case before them.

The Baskerville Mill was built about 1836 adjacent to the Nottoway River on the Dinwiddie side. The mill was a vertical turbine mill and was used as

McKenney Planing Mill. John Beck started the McKenney Planing Mill in 1903, one of the first enterprises in town. Situated next to the railway, the mill cut and shipped an abundance of loblolly pine. *Courtesy Bank of McKenney.*

Baskerville Ice & Milling Company. Situated on the Nottoway River, the mill generated electricity for McKenney until the late 1930s. *Photo by author.*

a gristmill for flour, corn and other grains. Mr. Channing Baskerville Sr., a graduate of Virginia Polytechnic Institute in 1922, obtained an electrical engineering degree. He soon installed some electricity-generating equipment to supply the local McKenney residents from his mill. In 1933, he expanded and began supplying electricity to residents in the neighboring county. With the coming of REA power in 1942, his electrical generating venture was shut down for good.

In 1926, he started an ice-making plant within the mill, using an ammonia compressor run off the engine. Ice would be supplied in one-hundred-pound blocks. The process was discontinued around the 1950s, when home refrigerators became popular. All the while, he continued managing the gristmill there as well. The mill has withstood two major floods and can still be seen off Route 40 on Baskerville Mill Road, just northwest of the town of McKenney.

During the Korean War, Captain William C. Wallace, of Dinwiddie, was awarded the Distinguished Service Cross for extraordinary heroism in connection with military operations against an armed enemy of the United Nations while serving as commanding officer of Company B, First Battalion, Ninth Infantry Regiment and Second Infantry Division. Captain Wallace distinguished himself by extraordinary heroism in action against enemy aggressor forces in the vicinity of Kunu-ri, Korea, on November 25, 1950. On that date, Company B was given the mission of attacking Hill 219, which was

> *occupied by a well-entrenched, numerically superior enemy force. To reach the objective it was necessary to take three knolls immediately in front of the enemy's position. Fighting with grim determination under the gallant leadership of Captain Wallace, the lead platoon took the first two knolls but was pinned down as they approached the third. Fully exposing himself to the deadly fire, Captain Wallace threw grenades into the enemy positions, enabling the remainder of his company to execute a flanking movement and seize the third knoll. Although painfully wounded in the face during this action, he again exposed himself to enemy fire, secured tank support and personally directed fire on the enemy strong points, inflicting heavy casualties and enabling his company to take the objective. Captain Wallace was subsequently wounded in action again on February 11, 1951, and was evacuated to the United States for treatment.*

Dinwiddie County has made a significant investment in athletics, with several youths obtaining athletic scholarships and a handful of them appearing on sports trading cards. In 1984–85, Dinwiddie's Larry Blackwell, outfielder, played for the Elizabethton, a Class AA team. Then in 1986, he played for the Kenosha, and in 1987–88, he played for the Visalia, having his highest batting average of .286 that year. In 1987, he played for the Orlando Twins, affiliate of the Minnesota Twins. On May 2, 1988, at Reno, he had seven runs batted in (RBI), bringing up a total of forty-seven RBIs that year for Visalia. Next at bat was Dinwiddie's Mike Mallory who, in 2001, made it to play baseball for the Lansing Lugnuts, a Class AA team. Then in 2004, Mallory played for the West Tennessee Diamond Jaxx.

As in any community, some days are darker than others and remembered even longer. In June 2005, a Dinwiddie County sheriff's deputy was killed after officials say a fifteen-year-old he was transporting from a court appearance shot him multiple times with his own gun. Fifty-nine-year-old Lieutenant James Weaver died at VCU Medical Center. The *Richmond Times-Dispatch* reported that the incident happened around 1:30 p.m. on Monday, June 27, near Crater Road and Interstate 95 in Petersburg. Police told the newspaper that Weaver was returning the teen to the Crater Juvenile Detention Center from a court appearance. But during the ride, the two began struggling. The teen endured one gunshot wound before grabbing Weaver's gun and shooting the officer an unspecified number of times. Police say the teen escaped on foot into a nearby apartment but came out ninety minutes later after his father called and talked him into surrendering. He faced a capital-murder charge, among other charges.

The consequences of the Vietnam War, Operation Desert Storm and Operation Enduring Freedom have been felt by many families living in Dinwiddie County. Given the recent decades of war, nearly every day a Dinwiddie veteran can be found traveling to the Hunter Holmes McGuire VA Medical Center in Richmond for care. The sadness and loss caused by all these wars is simply immeasurable.

June 5, 2006, was a very special day for Bank of McKenney. It was the one-hundred-year anniversary of the bank. To commemorate the occasion, the bank rang the closing bell of the NASDAQ stock exchange in New York City. It was quite an honor for a community bank, and the opportunity brought substantial media attention, but the recognition and overnight popularity didn't change the heart of the bank's purpose. President Richard M. Liles said, "At times such as this, I'm reminded of how important the personal service dimension of community banking truly is. With dedicated employees, loyal investors and supportive customers, we hope to continue into another century of banking excellence."

Left: Mr. William R. McKenney. The town of McKenney was named after the attorney for the Richmond, Petersburg and Carolina Railroad who worked for the Seaboard Air Line Railway and lived in Petersburg. *Courtesy Bank of McKenney.*

Below: B.T. Hargrave Feed Store. *Author's photo.*

Long-standing small businesses are scattered all over the county, such as Ragdales Building Supplies, a small female- and minority-owned business, which has been in the building and home improvement industry since 1972. B.T. Hargrave Feed Store sells horse, poultry, rabbit, goat, wildlife and exotic feeds and anything one may need for a healthy harvest. Giuseppe's Pizza has become a local family landmark for lunch and dinner along historic U.S. Route 1, near the Virginia Motorsports Park, while Brothers Pizza Italian Restaurant is a popular eatery on Cox Road in the Edgehill area of Dinwiddie County. Then there's El Caporal Mexican Restaurant on Route 460, which is becoming a popular eatery near the Dinwiddie Airport between the Wal-Mart and Amazon.Com Distribution Center. For a more complete current listing, contact the Dinwiddie Chamber of Commerce.

Dinwiddie has a great quality of life and a strong set of community values. Most Dinwiddie children attend modern public and private schools or are homeschooled in a community setting that affords them the benefits of a superior education. In general, Dinwiddie cares about the relationships that connect community, students and parents to our public school division. These relationships are the basis for the core values our county prides itself on: honesty, respect and integrity. Dinwiddie graduates have become soldiers, sailors, teachers, doctors, nurses, local business owners, bank executives, computer specialists, farmers, lawyers, CPAs, law enforcement officers, realtors, bricklayers, carpenters and contractors, culinary specialists and pharmacists, and the list goes on. In this age of great technological change and as we move toward a greater global economy—for better or worse—keeping our history and heritage will become that much more important to us.

Being just south of Richmond, Dinwiddie County is between the historic Nottoway and Appomattox Rivers. Here America was, in part, born; the final major campaign of the Civil War was fought; and the successful fight for civil rights was waged and won. Icons of American history left their footprints here. But while most visitors come to learn about America's past, many have also discovered the region's outstanding arts scene, outdoor recreation, shopping, antiques, dining and accommodations.

A vibrant heritage, beautiful natural resources and wonderful people make Dinwiddie County unique. It has what few locations in the United States have today: accessibility by two interstates and rail, as well as a high quality

Carson is home to the second-oldest branch of the Bank of Southside Virginia (BSV). It began as the Bank of Carson in 1911 and, in 1933, merged with the Bank of Stony Creek (started in 1905) and the Prince George County Bank (opened in 1919) to form the Bank of Southside Virginia. The Bank of Southside Virginia now has fifteen branches. It is said that Carson got its name from a telegram sent during a train derailment that read "cars off cars on." This photo was taken in Prince George County looking into Dinwiddie County across the railroad tracks. *Author's photo.*

of life, low cost of living and a diversely qualified and educated workforce. Plus, the Dinwiddie Airport and Industrial Park, along with the Dinwiddie Commerce Park, provides resources to future county-wide development. With Historic U.S. Route 1 running though the county, which extends from Maine to Key West, Florida, running parallel alongside I-95 and I-85, and U.S. Route 460 bisecting the county, few locations throughout the East Coast can boast greater accessibility. Dinwiddie's proximity to Virginia's capital city of Richmond positions it just minutes from the Port of Richmond, Central Virginia's domestic and international multi-modal freight and distribution gateway on the James River, serving waterborne, rail and truck shippers.

Hopefully this work will aid the citizens of Dinwiddie County to fully recognize the potential for tourism that historic resources create within a locality. The importance of protecting and preserving local historic properties, districts and open space could be seen as central to the county's heritage tourism efforts and as key components of economic growth. The preservation of historic buildings and districts attracts tourists and new business and can create new jobs, resulting in economic benefits for the community. The message of the economic benefits of historic preservation should be clearly expressed in the county's preservation planning programs and publications and in the county's economic development materials. Dinwiddie County is fortunate to have the professional resources of the

Virginia Department of Historic Resources, Virginia Historical Society and the Library of Virginia and their outstanding archives, collections and research libraries available to us all.

ATTRACTIONS EVERY VISITOR SHOULD FIND OF INTEREST

Civil Rights in Education Heritage Trail

Our nation's free public education system was born here in Southside Virginia. It was along the sleepy back roads of a few rural counties that African Americans, Native Americans and women earned the right to an education that was equal to that given to white males. A self-guided driving tour highlights forty-one of these historically significant sites and tells the poignant and often explosive story of civil rights in American education. Nine of the forty-one sites are located in Chesterfield County, Petersburg County and Dinwiddie County. Because the trail is not linear or chronological, it can be started and ended at any point. Once you begin, follow the Civil Rights in Education Trail signs from one stop to the next. A Virginia state map could be helpful if you want to skip a stop or if you should get lost. Pick one up at any Virginia Welcome Center or call 1-804-786-2801 to receive one by mail. To fully experience the tour, allow time to enter buildings that are publicly accessible; it will take approximately two full days. A free brochure and map are available online at www.varetreat.com or by calling 1-800-6-RETREAT.

Lake Chesdin

Lake Chesdin (aka Chesdin Reservoir) is conveniently located near Richmond in central Virginia, along the Dinwiddie County line with Chesterfield. The reservoir is an impoundment of the Appomattox River created by Brasfield Dam. At 3,100 acres, there is room to roam in search of a wide variety of fish species, including largemouth bass, both black and white crappie, channel catfish and modest populations of walleye and striped bass. A fish lift to give anatropous fish like shad and herring access to the upper river is in place. Marinas and boat launches include Cozy Cove Marina,

713 Sutherland Road, Church Road, 23833 (Dinwiddie County), 804-265-9000; Whippernock Marina and Campground, 2700 Sutherland Road, Sutherland, 23885 (Dinwiddie County), 804-265-5252; and the public boat ramp at Chesdin Road, near the dam. The ramp is open twenty-four hours a day, with a handicap-accessible fishing pier.

Lee's Retreat Civil War Driving Tour

The trail is composed of twenty-six posted stops from Petersburg to Appomattox Courthouse National Historical Park with detailed audio and visual interpretation at each site. The self-guided driving tour allows you to enjoy the trail at your own pace. It is suggested you start the trail in Petersburg at South Side Railroad Station to experience the trail in chronological order. However, many people enjoy following it backward from Appomattox. Follow the Lee's Retreat trail-blazing signs from one stop to the next. A Lee's Retreat brochure and a Virginia state map could be helpful if you want to skip a stop. Pick them up at any Virginia Welcome Center or call 1-800-6-RETREAT to receive them by mail. A downloadable map is also available at www.varetreat.com.

Lucky Lake Mining Gem and Mineral Mine

This attraction offers something for everyone, from the amateur to the advanced rock collector. Here, you'll find treasures to last a lifetime! Partially covered handicapped-accessible flume and screening material provided. Wear old clothes that can get wet and dirty. Have stones graded and cut by the professional gemologist and stonecutter. There is a picnic area and gift shop with gemstones, rocks, minerals and jewelry from around the world. It is located at 4125 Harpers Road in McKenney. Call for hours: 804-478-5468, or visit www.luckylakeva.com.

Pamplin Historical Park and the National Museum of the Civil War Soldier

This 422-acre campus features four award-winning museums, four historic homes, costumed living history demonstrations, guided tours and the Breakthrough Battlefield of April 2, 1865. The park's facilities and programs appeal to casual visitors, serious students of Civil War–era history and families alike. Pamplin Historical Park's acclaimed National Museum of the Civil War Soldier features the stories of thirteen soldiers, including black soldier Sergeant Alexander H. Newton, of the Twenty-ninth Connecticut Infantry. At age seventy-two, Newton published his autobiography *Out of the Briars*, which offers an excellent glimpse of his early years in the South and his experiences as a soldier in the Union army. The Field Quarter is one of America's finest slave life exhibits. Reproduction cabins, outbuildings and a garden simulate the meager living conditions of field slaves and their families. A frame cabin houses the thought-provoking video *Slavery in America: Viewpoints of the 1850s*, which illustrates some of the common opinions Americans held about slavery. At the Banks House, visitors may experience the rare opportunity to view an original slave structure. The kitchen and slave quarter date to the 1840s and served as a kitchen, laundry and living quarters for house slaves and their families. Pamplin Historical Park has received accolades from a wide range of national and regional media and has been rated by AAA Automotive Club as a "Gem Attraction." It is located at 6125 Boydton Plank Road, Petersburg, 23803; call 1-877-PAMPLIN, or visit www.pamplinpark.org.

Petersburg National Battlefield—Five Forks Unit

By the spring of 1865, the last remaining supply line into Petersburg was the South Side Railroad. On March 29, 1865, Grant sent his forces on a westward movement to cut this major artery, knowing that it would cause Lee to abandon Petersburg and Richmond. Countering this move, Lee sent ten thousand troops, under Major General George E. Pickett, to an important road junction called Five Forks, which protected the railroad. On April 1, twenty-two thousand Union troops, under Major General Philip H. Sheridan, attacked and defeated Pickett's force at Five Forks. The fall of Richmond was assured. This site is located at 16302 White Oak Road, Church Road.

Sutherland Station/Historic Fork Inn

Confederates fought for the doomed South Side Railroad here on April 2, 1865. The building just beyond the Lee's Retreat wayside is the Historic Fork Inn, a restored fourteen-room 1803 plantation house. The house served as a Union army hospital and later as one of southern Virginia's

This picture was taken by NPS staff in October 2009 during the grand opening for the new Five Forks Visitor Contact Station. Seasonal NPS employee Bill Backus brought some friends in to do a firing demonstration. *Courtesy NPS Petersburg.*

Virginia Motorsports Park. *Courtesy of Virginia Motorsports Park (VMP).*

first post offices. Furnishings are from the eighteenth and early nineteenth centuries. Civil War memorabilia includes weapons, personal items, clothing, medical instruments and a Confederate soldier's wooden leg. It is located at 19621 Namozine Road, Sutherland, 23885. Call 804-265-8141 for more information. (Dinwiddie County; Stop #3 on Lee's Retreat Driving Tour.)

Virginia Motorsports Park

This state-of-the-art, five-hundred-acre facility is the home to some of the country's hottest racing action, including drag racing, mud bog, motocross, autocross, truck and tractor pulls and a family ATV park. The park has become known as one of the top drag race strips in the nation. Built for speed, Virginia Motorsports Park was constructed in 1994 to showcase the most exciting motorsports events with the fastest racecars in the world. The quarter-mile drag strip is home to a variety of drag racing events featuring dragsters, funny cars, jet cars, street rods, motorcycles and monster trucks. It seats twenty-three thousand spectators and has 60 acres of pit space. The park hosts specialty events such as the Super Chevy Show, Fun Ford Weekend, Nite of Fire and the East Coast Truckin' Nationals. The park also features a weekly drag racing program in which racers from all over Virginia, Maryland and North Carolina compete. The mud bog is home to some of the dirtiest action in racing. Its two tracks feature over two hundred feet of mud-slinging challenges. The new family all-terrain vehicle (ATV) park offers over 250 acres of riding space, a pavilion, picnic area, snack bar and showers. There are three trails for all skill levels. Bring your own ATV or rent a machine at the park. All in all, it's a great place for sun, fun and food as the hottest ground-shaking cars hit the strip at the Virginia Motorsports Park. The park is located at 8018 Boydton Plank Road (U.S. Route 1), Petersburg, 23803. For a schedule of events, facility information and admission prices, call 804-862-3174, or go to www.virginiamotorsports.com.

Wilson-Kautz Raid Civil War Driving Tour

This trail is composed of twenty-six stops with detailed interpretation at each site. The self-guided driving tour allows you to enjoy the trail at your own pace. Because the trail is not linear or chronological, it can be started and ended at any point. Once you begin, follow the Virginia Civil War Trails trail-blazing signs from one stop to the next. A Lee's Retreat brochure and a Virginia state map could be helpful if you want to skip a stop or should you get lost. Pick them up at any Virginia Welcome Center or call 1-800-6-RETREAT to receive them by mail. A downloadable map is also available at www.varetreat.com. To fully experience the tour, allowing time to enter buildings that are publicly accessible, will take approximately two full days. Petersburg Trading Co., Inc., is located at 5927 Boydton Plank Road (U.S. Route 1).

Petersburg Visitors Center (Farmers' Bank)

One of the nation's only bank museums, the Farmers' Bank was incorporated in 1812 and opened its Petersburg branch in 1817. The three-story Federal structure became a frequent gathering place for the Petersburg community. The first floor of the building held the banking area with the original vault. Clerks cashed checks and made exchanges from the other side of a long counter. In the early nineteenth century, the executive officer of the bank and his family lived on the upper floors of the bank. The rooms were well appointed with intricately decorated mantels and doorways. A family kitchen has been built on its original site. The bank continued to operate through the Civil War. In 1866, the General Assembly passed an act that affected all state banks and forced the Farmers' Bank to liquidate its assets. The bank became a private residence and passed through many hands before being conveyed to Preservation Virginia (then the Association for the Preservation of Virginia Antiquities) in 1960. The first floor is now exhibited as a bank. Located at 19 Bollingbrook Street, Petersburg, the center can be reached by phone at 804-733-2400. The Petersburg City website for the Petersburg Visitors Center can be found at http://www.petersburg-va.org/tourism.

Petersburg Area Information Center

This visitor rest stop located on I-95 northbound provides information for the attractions in Petersburg and, as a welcome center, has information for destinations throughout the Petersburg area and the state. For more regional info, see the PART website at www.PetersburgArea.org.

The Siege Museum at 15 West Bank Street, Petersburg

"The key to taking Richmond is Petersburg," declared Union general Ulysses S. Grant when his forces arrived at the eastern environs of Petersburg in mid-June 1864. Petersburg's five railroad lines and key roadways made it an important target. If the Union forces cut those transportation routes, Petersburg could no longer provide Richmond and Lee's army with much-needed supplies, equipment and subsistence. Many believed that if Richmond fell, the war would be over. The road to Petersburg began in May as Grant's 122,000-man army crossed the Rapidan River near Fredericksburg and engaged Lee's 65,000 troops in a series of hard-fought battles.

For a month, the two armies clashed, marched and clashed again. After each encounter, Grant moved farther southward and closer to his goals: the destruction of Lee's army and the Confederate capital of Richmond. As Grant's larger force pressed Richmond from the north, his smaller Army of the James landed at Bermuda Hundred in eastern Chesterfield County and pushed inland toward the capital from the south. Confederate troops desperately defended the approaches to Richmond in a series of battles and, on May 16, launched a counterattack that staggered the Union forces and forced them back to Bermuda Hundred. By the beginning of June, the Union's larger force camped within nine miles of the capital, but Lee still blocked its way. At Cold Harbor on June 3, Grant tried a frontal assault to crush the Confederate army and enter Richmond. The Union forces suffered a disastrous defeat that convinced Grant to abandon plans to capture Richmond by direct assault. Instead, he moved his forces south across the James River and through Prince George County. On June 15, he threw them against Petersburg's eastern front. In a grim ten-month struggle—the longest siege in American warfare—Grant's army gradually but relentlessly isolated Petersburg and cut Lee's supply lines from the south. The two armies dug elaborate defensive positions from which they fought, sometimes only yards apart, in a grim precursor to the trench warfare of World War I. For the outnumbered Confederates, it was months of desperately hanging on, hoping the people of the North would tire of the war.

General Grant made his headquarters at City Point (today's Hopewell), a small port town at the confluence of the James and Appomattox Rivers eight miles northeast of Petersburg. Overnight, the tiny village became one of the busiest ports in the world as hundreds of ships unloaded equipment and supplies that the Union army used to wear down the Confederates. Throughout the siege, Petersburg's residents endured the danger of shelling and the pain of hunger as supplies slowed to a trickle. Lavish lifestyles in the years prior to the war gave way to a bitter struggle for survival. A chicken could sell for fifty dollars in Confederate scrip. Sitting hens were stolen from their nests. Clothing, shoes and firewood became prized commodities.

On July 30, while at his headquarters at Violet Bank (in what is today the city of Colonial Heights), General Lee received word of the war's most spectacular event. In an attempt to punch a hole in Petersburg's defenses, Union soldiers tunneled under Confederate earthworks and exploded eight thousand pounds of gunpowder. The massive explosion at the Battle of the Crater instantly killed and wounded 278 Confederates, but the Union charge failed and trench warfare resumed.

Over the next several months, a series of vicious battles in Dinwiddie County forced Lee to extend his thinly manned lines for thirty-seven miles in an arc below Petersburg. As his army crept south and west, Grant slowly gained possession of all the key rail lines except the South Side Railroad. By mid-March 1865, Lee understood that Grant's superior force would either go around the Confederate right flank or pierce the line somewhere along its length. With victory near, Grant unleashed General Philip H. Sheridan at Five Forks on April 1. His objective: the South Side Railroad. Sheridan smashed the Confederate forces under George Pickett and the next day gained access to the tracks beyond. On April 2, Grant ordered an all-out assault, and Lee's right flank crumbled at what is now Pamplin Historical Park, in Dinwiddie County. A valiant defense at Confederate Fort Gregg, in Dinwiddie County, slowed the Union advance and spared General Lee from possible street fighting in Petersburg. On the night of April 2, his army evacuated Petersburg by slipping north across the Appomattox River. Petersburg's citizens now realized their greatest fears as Union troops marched in unimpeded and occupied the city. The back door to Richmond had been opened, and the capital quickly fell to Union forces. Lee surrendered to Grant at Appomattox Courthouse just one week later. As Grant had predicted, Petersburg had been the key.

The Siege Museum tells this tale and many more, and the museum can be reached by phone at 804-733-2404.

Centre Hill Museum—A Showcase of Gracious Southern Living and Style

For several years on the evening of January 24, residents of Centre Hill heard what they believed to be ghosts of Civil War soldiers marching up and down the home's staircase. A popular ghost watch is held annually on that date. Built in 1823 by Robert Bolling IV, Centre Hill remained an opulent Petersburg residence until 1936. It is often described as a symbol of the grandeur of nineteenth-century Virginia aristocracy. The home's interior features outstanding examples of Greek Revival, Federal and Colonial Revival architecture. During a guided tour, you will learn about the mansion's history, including its role during the Civil War and visits by Presidents Abraham Lincoln and William Howard Taft. You will also see decorative arts, memorabilia and photographs from the mansion's archives. A nominal admission fee is charged, and there is a gift and bookshop on site. Located at 1 Center Hill Avenue, Petersburg, 23803, the museum can be reached at 804-733-2401 or www.petersburg-va.org/tourism/cntrhill.htm.

Battersea

Built in 1768 on the banks of the Appomattox River in Dinwiddie County for Colonel John Banister, Petersburg's first mayor, Revolutionary War Patriot and framer of the Articles of Confederation, Battersea is an important colonial urban villa. It is built in the neo-Palladian style that was popularized in England in the eighteenth century and embraced in colonial Virginia, and it features a spectacular Chinese Chippendale staircase. Each year on the third weekend in April, Battersea is the setting of a commemorative reenactment of the Battle of Petersburg. For more details, see http://batterseafound.org/. The villa is open for tours by appointment and located at 1289 Upper Appomattox Street, Petersburg, 23803. Call 804-733-2400, or visit www.petersburg-va.org.

Blandford Church and Cemetery

This is indeed a rare American treasure. It is one of the few churches whose decorative stained-glass windows were completely executed under the direction of the famous designer Louis Comfort Tiffany of New York.

Battersea Revolutionary War reenactment. *Author's collection.*

Blandford. *Author's collection.*

The church's fifteen exquisite windows were commissioned by the Ladies' Memorial Association of Petersburg in memory of the Confederate soldiers buried at the adjacent Blandford Cemetery. From 1901 to 1912, Tiffany and his team of artists designed, created and installed the windows, which were financed by contributions from each of the Confederate states in honor of their war dead. A guided tour of the church reveals its history as an eighteenth-century Anglican house of worship, its eventual abandonment and fall into disrepair, its use as a field hospital during the Siege of Petersburg and its restoration by the Ladies' Memorial Association as a shrine to the South's "Lost Cause." You will also learn the story behind each window's design and experience the amazing artistry, harmony and proportion of Tiffany's work.

Your tour then takes you into Blandford Cemetery, one of the oldest and largest in America. It is the resting place of an estimated thirty thousand Confederate soldiers who lost their lives during the Siege of Petersburg. You will learn about the interment of the Confederate dead and see outstanding examples of eighteenth-, nineteenth- and twentieth-century gravestones, sculptures and decorative iron fences. An admission fee is charged, and there is a gift and bookshop on-site. It is located on Rochelle Lane (off Crater Road) in Petersburg, 23803. Call 804-733-2396 or 804-458-4682, or visit http://www.petersburg-va.org/blandford/index.asp.

Petersburg: The Underground Railroad and the Struggle for Freedom

This brochure and walking tour map is a guide to discovering twenty-eight sites in Old Towne Petersburg tied to African American history and the Underground Railroad. Among the highlights is the former home of slave Elizabeth Keckley, who became Mary Todd Lincoln's seamstress and closest friend. She toured Petersburg with President and Mrs. Lincoln just days before the president was assassinated in Washington, D.C. The brochure and map are available for free at the Petersburg Visitor Center in Old Towne or by calling 804-733-2400.

The National Park Service's Petersburg National Battlefield

This 2,700-acre park preserves and interprets the sites of the 9½-month-long Siege of Petersburg. A brochure titled "African-Americans at Petersburg" highlights the actions of the 850 slaves and free blacks who helped build the Confederate fortifications around Petersburg and the 7,800 U.S. Colored Troops who fought and died in the campaign, including the famous Battle of the Crater. Most who died are buried at the Park Service's Poplar Grove National Cemetery in Dinwiddie County.

Butterworth's farm at harvest time. A young Raymond Poole stands at its rear. *Courtesy of Butterworth family.*

The second courthouse burned in 1821. A new frame courthouse was built soon after but only lasted until 1849, when the historic Dinwiddie County Courthouse was built on the same tract. The village that grew up around the courthouse resembled other small county seats of a similar date in possessing a single square lined with houses and businesses, including the centrally placed courthouse and a nearby tavern to accommodate the court and its clients during a period of several days each month.

Built in 1851, the Dinwiddie County Courthouse was the headquarters of Union general Philip H. Sheridan during the Battle of Dinwiddie and the Battle of Five Forks. The Union's victory at Five Forks led to the capture of Lee's last railroad supply line into Petersburg and the eventual fall of the city. The adjacent Calvary Episcopal Church was used as a hospital by the First Maine Cavalry. Markers commemorate battles fought in the county and ten unknown Union soldiers buried in the churchyard. The courthouse was active through 1998 and is now home to the Dinwiddie County Historical Society. The building is located 14101 Boydton Plank Road, Dinwiddie, 23841, PO Box 153. Please visit http://dinwiddiehistory.org/index.html for more information.

BIBLIOGRAPHY

Biographical Directory of the U.S. Congress 1774–Present.

Chataigne, J.H. *Chataigne's Virginia Gazeteer and Classified Business Directory, 1888–89*. Richmond: J.H. Chataigne and Co., 1888.

———. *Chataigne's Virginia Gazeteer and Classified Business Directory, 1890–91*. Richmond, VA: J.H. Chataigne and Co., 1890.

———. *Virginia Business Directory and Gazetteer and Richmond City Directory, 1877–78*. Richmond, VA: J.W. Rudolf and English, 1877.

Davis, Robert P., et al. *Virginia Presbyterians in American Life: Hanover Presbytery (1755–1980)*. Richmond, VA: Hanover Presbytery, 1982.

Dinwiddie County Heritage Book Committee. Dinwiddie County Heritage 1752–2006. Waynesville, NC: County Heritage Inc., 2006.

Dinwiddie County Virginia Court Order Book 1789–1791. *Virginia Genealogical Society Quarterly Bulletin* 5, no. 1 (January 1966).

Edwards, Richard. *A Statistical Gazeteer of Virginia*. Richmond, VA: published for the proprietor, 1855.

Eggleston, J.D., Jr. "A Contrast: A Word to Superintendents, Trustees, and Folks Generally." *Virginia Journal of Education* (June 1910): 610–12.

Elliot and Nye's Virginia Directory and Business Register, 1852.

Ewan, J. & W. Ewan. *John Banister and His Natural History of Virginia 1678–1692*. Champaign: University of Illinois Press, 1970.:

Glassie, Henry. *Folk Housing in Middle Virginia*. Knoxville: University of Tennessee Press, 1975.

Hamilton, Phillip. *The Making and Unmaking of a Revolutionary Family: The Tuckers of Virginia, 1752–1830*. Charlottesville: University of Virginia Press, 2003, 2008.

Herringshaw, Thomas William. *Herringshaw's National Library of American Biography*. Transcribed by Therman Kellar. Chicago: American Publisher's Association, 1909.

Hughes, Sarah S. *Surveyors and Statesmen: Land Measuring in Colonial Virginia*. N.p.: Virginia Surveyors Foundation, Virginia Association of Surveyors, 1979.

The Jamestown Exhibit Committee of Dinwiddie Co. Virginia. *Historic Dinwiddie County, Virginia or the Last Long Camp*. Petersburg, VA: Franklin Press, 1907.

Jones, Richard L. *Dinwiddie County: Carrefour of the Commonwealth*. Dinwiddie, VA: Dinwiddie County Historical Book Committee, 1976.

Loth, Calder. *The Virginia Landmarks Register*. Charlottesville: University Press of Virginia, 1987.

Meacham, Sarah Hand. *Every Home a Distillery: Alcohol, Gender, and Technology in the Colonial Chesapeake*. Baltimore, Maryland: Johns Hopkins University Press, 2009.

Melton, Herman. *Southside Virginia: Echoing Through History*. Charleston, SC: The History Press, 2006.

Peters, John O., and Margaret Peters. *Virginia's Historic Courthouses*. Charlottesville: University Press of Virginia, 1995.

Seagrave, Ronald. *The Early Artisans and Mechanics of Petersburg, Virginia, 1607–1860*. Parker, CO: Outskirts Press, 2009, 2011.

Semple, Robert B. *A History of the Rise and Progress of the Baptists in Virginia: 1810*. Richmond, VA: Pitt and Dickenson, 1894.

Slave Narratives: A Folk History of Slavery in the United States from Interviews with Former Slaves, North Carolina Narratives. Vol. XI, Part 2. Vol. XI, Publ. 1941. The Federal Writers' Project, 1936–1938. Library of Congress.

A Survey of Historic Architecture in Dinwiddie County, Virginia conducted for Virginia Department of Historic Resources, Richmond, Virginia and the Dinwiddie County Planning Department, 2010.

Thomson's Mercantile and Professional Directory for Delaware, Maryland, Virginia and North Carolina, 1851–52. Baltimore, MD: William Thomson, 1851.

Trout, W.E. *The Appomattox River Atlas Historic Sites on the Appomattox and Its Navigable Branches*. Covesville, VA: Virginia Canal & Navigation Society, 2003.

Virginia General Assembly. Petitions. Files of the Library of Virginia.

Willoughby, Laura. *Petersburg*. Charleston, SC: Arcadia Publishing, 2006.

Worrall, Jay, Jr. *The Friendly Virginians: America's First Quakers*. Athens, GA: Iberian Publishing Co., 1994.

Writers' Program of the Works Progress Administration. *Dinwiddie County: The Country of Apamatica*. Richmond, VA: Whittet and Shepperson, 1942.

Zehmer, J. "The Early Domestic Architecture of Dinwiddie County, Virginia." Master's thesis, University of Virginia, 1970.

HISTORIC MAPS OF THE AREA

Campbell, A.H. Map of Dinwiddie County, for the Confederate government. 1864.

———. Map of Goochland County. Confederate Engineer's Office. June 1863.

Hargrave, Isham E. A Correct Map of Dinwiddie County. 1820.

Rives, T.F. Map of the County of 1878.

Wood, James. Map of Dinwiddie County. 1820.

INDEX

C

G

H

Q

R

S

ABOUT THE AUTHOR

Author Ronald Roy Seagrave is an independent scholar, historian and award-winning author and lecturer. In early 2006, he received a "gift of life" as a liver transplant recipient. He is an active volunteer for UNOS, the United Network for Organ Sharing, in Richmond. He is also an active member of the Society of Civil War Historians, City of Petersburg Sesquicentennial Committee, the Virginia Historical Society and Virginia Museum of Fine Art. The Petersburg Historic Foundation awarded him with its Historic Heritage Award in 2010, for his groundbreaking work entitled *The Early Artisans and Mechanics of Petersburg, 1607–1860*.